THE BOOK OF
CRAFTS

THE BOOK OF
CRAFTS

this edition produced exclusively for

WHSMITH

Produced specially for
W.H. Smith & Sons
by Pan Books Ltd
Cavaye Place
London SW10 9PG
© Pan Books Ltd 1979

ISBN 0 330 25895 8

Typesetting by Crawley Composition
Printed by Cripplegate Printing
Company Limited

CONTENTS

EMBROIDERY

Equipment

The few items needed for needlework should be of the highest quality to ensure the best results. Keep them neatly arranged in a specially-designed sewing box.

Needles. Long-eyed and sharp-pointed needles known as 'crewel' are best for embroidery on fabric; blunt-pointed needles are available for canvas work and darning techniques. Keep a good selection of needles in a flannel book to prevent rusting. Select the size of needle according to the thickness of thread and fabric; for example, a size 7 crewel needle for 3 strands of embroidery thread on a medium-weight fabric, and size 18 tapestry needle for tapestry wool on a medium-weight canvas.
The needle must carry the thread through the fabric without distorting it. Never use a bent needle, as this will result in uneven stitching.

Pins. Use steel pins to avoid rust marks in the fabric.

Thimble. This must be well made and a comfortable fit. The surface should be chased to stop the needle from slipping and the thimble should be steel-lined to prevent the needle from penetrating it.

Scissors. Embroidery scissors should have small, narrow blades with sharp points. If a sheath is not available, use a cork to protect the points of the scissors.
Use larger and heavier scissors to cut fabric and thick wool.

Carbon. There is a special non-smudge carbon for transferring embroidery designs to fabric. Use light or dark carbon, depending on the colour of the fabric being used.

Transfer pencils. Obtainable from art needlework departments, these are needed when re-using transfers and for drawing over traced patterns.

Threads. Stranded cotton can be divided up into the thickness required. It is useful to have a shade card to select the most suitable colours. Coton à broder and pearl cotton are good for all-over patterns such as cutwork.
Use tacking thread for basting.

Frames. Stitching is more even when fabric is held taut by an embroidery frame. There are several types of frame, and the choice depends on the kind of needlework. Round wooden frames are best suited to fine work; use square frames for heavier work. Frames are available on floor stands, too, freeing both hands for working.

Fabric. Always choose firmly woven fabric so that it will hold the stitching well and withstand wear and tear, thereby justifying your efforts.

General hints

1. Always cut embroidery threads; breaking them causes stretching and results in uneven work.

2. Use short lengths of thread when embroidering to prevent the surface from becoming scuffed by the continuous pulling through the fabric in stitching.

3. Do not use knots to anchor thread. Run the needle in and out of the fabric and cover these running-stitches with embroidery.

4. To end off a thread, run the needle through completed stitches on the wrong side of the work.

5. Practise new stitches until they are perfect before including them in a piece of needlework.

6. Do not use unravelled thread for embroidery; it gives an uneven result.

7. Make a cushion pad about 2.5cm (1in) larger all round than the cushion cover itself to give well-filled corners.

8. Cover worked sections with tissue to prevent soiling and rubbing when work is in progress.

9. Before mounting work in a round embroidery frame, bind the inner ring of the frame with calico to ensure a firm hold on the fabric.

10. Use linen thread for lacing embroidery fabric to a square frame.

11. Wind metallic threads around a silk pad to prevent damage.

12. Store metallic threads in dark tissue to prevent discoloration.

13. Pad backing card with cotton wadding before mounting embroidery.

14. Do not use too many colours in one piece of needlework, and plan the entire piece before you start work.

15. Adapt designs from greetings cards and posters if you cannot draw patterns.

16. To enlarge a design, rule the pattern into squares not larger than about 2.5cm (1in). Take a piece of paper the size the design is to be enlarged to, and divide this into the same number of squares as the pattern. Now draw the pattern in on the larger paper, reproducing in each corresponding square the appropriate section of the pattern.

17. To use a pattern where only half of the repeat is given, trace the section provided on to tracing paper, fold the paper in two and then draw the pattern in reverse through the folded paper to complete the design. Use carbon paper to transfer the traced design to the fabric.

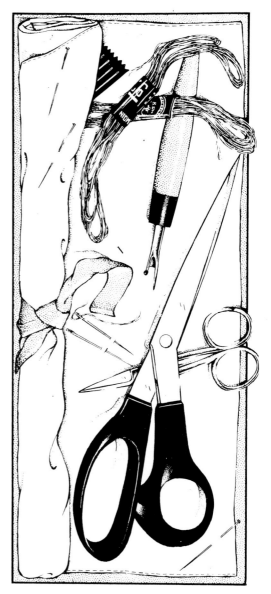

Stitches

Back-stitch. This consists of short, even stitches forming a continuous line on the surface and double-length stitches underneath. This stitch also makes a strong seam. Work from right to left. Insert needle to the right of the thread and bring it out an equal distance to the left of the thread.

Blanket-stitch. Work from left to right, making straight downward stitches with the thread under the needle to form the loop along the stitching line.

Bricking-stitch. The first row consists of long and short stitches over four and two threads alternately. The successive rows consist of straight-stitches worked over four threads and fitting evenly into the preceding row. Continue in this way, working the last row to correspond with the first.

Bullion-stitch. Insert the needle about 6mm ($\frac{1}{4}$in) to the right of the thread, bringing it out at the original point; wind thread round the needle four or five times, then re-insert the needle at the end of the stitch, holding the loops with the left thumb until the thread has been pulled taut to form the stitch.

Buttonhole-stitch. Work from left to right, keeping the stitches close together. Make straight downward stitches with the thread under the needle. Draw thread up to form loop along edge.

Ceylon-stitch. Work detached loop stitches loosely to resemble knitted fabric.

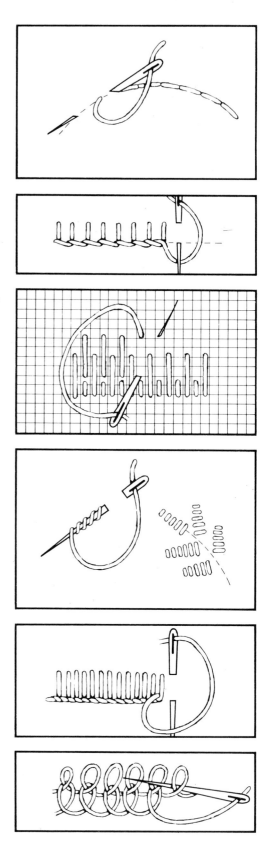

Chain-stitch. Hold the thread down with the left thumb. Insert the needle where the thread emerged, and bring it out over the looped thread as shown.

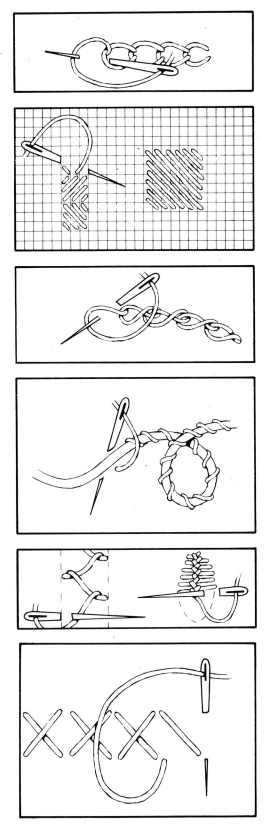

Chequerboard-stitch. Work diagonally over one, two, three, two, one crossings of canvas threads, then reverse the diagonal direction over the next threads. Continue in this way, alternating direction throughout the pattern. For larger patterns, work over one to six crossings of canvas threads.

Coral-stitch. Work from right to left. Hold the thread down with the left thumb. Insert the needle under the thread and through the fabric, then bring the needle out over the working thread.

Couching. Lay a thread along the line of the design and hold it down with the left hand. With another thread make tiny stitches at right-angles over the laid thread and through the fabric. Do not allow the laid thread to pucker and take the ends of the laid thread to the back of the work to fasten off. Any number of threads may be couched down.

Cretan-stitch. This stitch may be worked in a solid or an open style. Bring needle out over the looping thread from left to right alternately as shown.

Cross-stitch. Bring the needle out on the lower right line of the cross and insert it at the top of the same line; bring the needle out on the lower left line in position for the next stitch (a). Continue in this way for the number of stitches required and complete the second half of the cross-stitch on the return (b). It is important for the upper halves of the stitches to slant in the same direction.

Fly-stitch. This may be worked singly or in continuous lines as shown. Bring the needle out on the left; hold the thread with the left thumb, insert the needle on the same level to the right and bring it out lower down in the centre, over the working thread. Insert the needle again immediately below to secure the loop.

French-knot. Hold the thread down with the left thumb and twist the needle twice round the held thread. Still holding the thread, insert the needle back through the same place and draw the thread through the knot to the back of the work.

Hemming. Work from right to left. Insert the needle into the single fabric just below the fold and bring it out at an angle through the fold. Do not draw thread up too tightly.

Herringbone-stitch. Work from left to right. First take a stitch from right to left on the upper level, then take a similar stitch on the lower level and continue alternating stitches in this way throughout. See also threaded herringbone-stitch.

Lazy-daisy-stitch. This consists of loops fastened at the foot with small stitches.

Open-chain-stitch. This is worked on two parallel lines. Bring the thread out at top left. Hold the thread down with the left thumb and insert the needle at top right. Bring the needle out again at bottom left, leaving the loop thus formed slightly loose. Insert the needle at bottom right and bring it out over the looped thread in position for the next stitch.

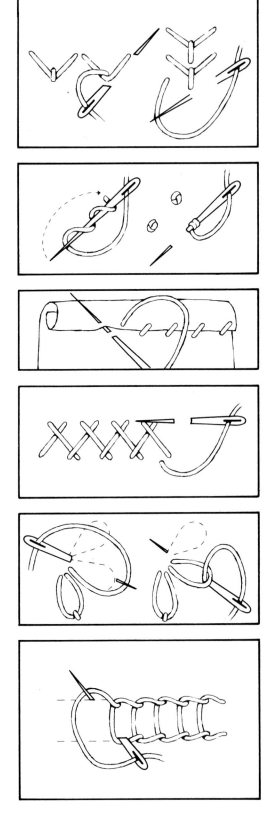

Open-cloud-stitch. Vandyke the threaded needle through these stitches to form surface patterns as shown.

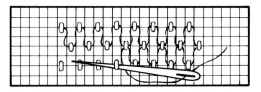

Overcast-stitch. Bring laid threads through fabric and hold with the left thumb. Bring the working thread through and work small satin-stitches closely over the laid threads, following the lines of the design. Take the laid threads through to the back of the fabric to finish.

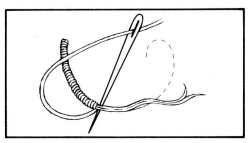

Oversewing. Work from right to left. Take the needle over the edge and insert it diagonally through both edges, keeping the stitches near the edge.

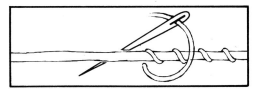

Rhodes-stitch. Bring the needle out at (a), insert it at (b), bring it out at (c), insert it at (d), bring it out at (e), insert it at (f). Continue in this way, following the direction of the arrows, and with each stitch overlapping the previous one, until square is filled.

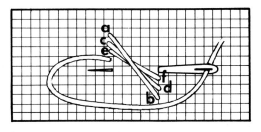

Running-stitch. This stitch is used for light seams and for gathering fabric. Work from right to left. Weave the needle in and out of fabric, feeding the fabric on to the needle point with the left hand. Make the stitches even on both sides of the fabric, easing fabric off the other end of the needle as work proceeds.

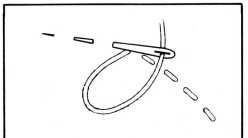

Satin-stitch. Work stitches evenly and close together so that they resemble satin. Take care in keeping edges even throughout.

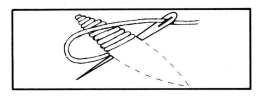

Seeding. Work tiny back-stitches in all directions as shown. Work over the same stitch more than once to give texture.

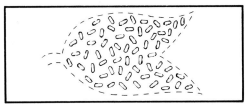

Slip-stitch. Work from right to left. Pick up a thread in the single fabric immediately below the fold, then slip needle along inside folded edge into position for the next stitch.

Spider's web. Begin with a fly-stitch to the centre of the circle as shown in (a), then work two straight-stitches, one on each side of the fly-stitch tail, into the centre of circle. This divides the circle into five equal sections and the 'spokes' form the foundation of the web. Weave needle over and under the 'spokes' as shown in (b) until the circle is filled.

Stab-stitch. This is used for sewing more than two layers together or when fabric is too thick for the needle to pass in and out in the one movement. Take the needle at a right-angle through all the layers from front to back of the work, then return the needle at a right-angle from back to front of the work, and continue in this way throughout.

Stem-stitch. Work from left to right. Insert the needle to the right and bring it out to the left in the centre of the stitch and keeping the working thread below the needle throughout.

Straight-stitch. The simplest stitch in embroidery, used to cover any straight lines as shown.

Threaded back-stitch. First work back-stitch. Pass the threaded needle up and down under the back-stitches without piercing the fabric. To do this easily, pass the threaded end, instead of the point, under the stitch, as shown.

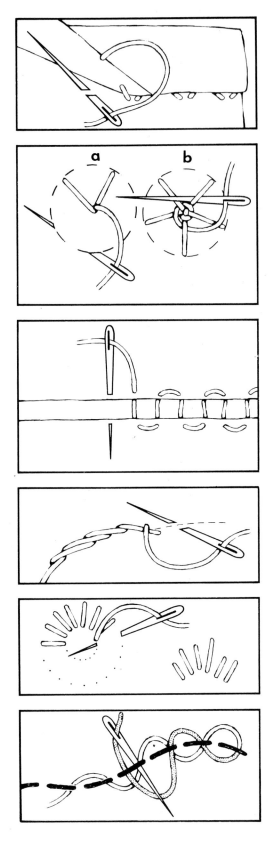

Threaded herringbone-stitch.
After working herringbone-stitch, take a contrasting thread and, using the blunt end of the needle, weave the thread under the stitches as shown.

Trellis-couching. Lay straight-stitches down and across the area, forming squares. Work a small stitch over each intersection to hold the threads in position.

Velvet-stitch. Leave tiny loops be-tween stitches – these loops may be cut if required. Cross-stitch secures the loops.

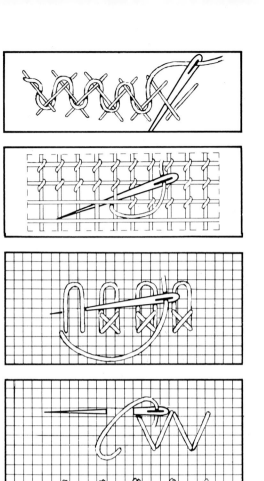

Wave-stitch. Work from right to left. Bring the thread through at the arrow; insert the needle at (a) and bring it out at (b). Insert the needle again at the arrow and bring the needle out at (c). Continue in this way throughout. Turn fabric round to work the second row as shown.

Wide gobelin-stitch. The first row is worked from left to right. Bring the needle out at arrow; insert two threads down and two threads to the left, draw the needle out two threads up and three threads to the right in position for the next stitch. Work the next row from right to left. Vary the number of threads worked over as shown in original.

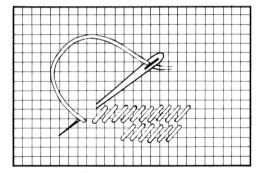

Zig-zag chain. Work loop-stitches to left and right alternately, bring-ing the needle out above the thread as shown.

Hungarian box

This is embroidered in traditional
bright colours on neutral crash.

An actual-size design for the embroidery is shown opposite. Use pearl
cotton and work the design in satin-
stitch and stem-stitch.

15

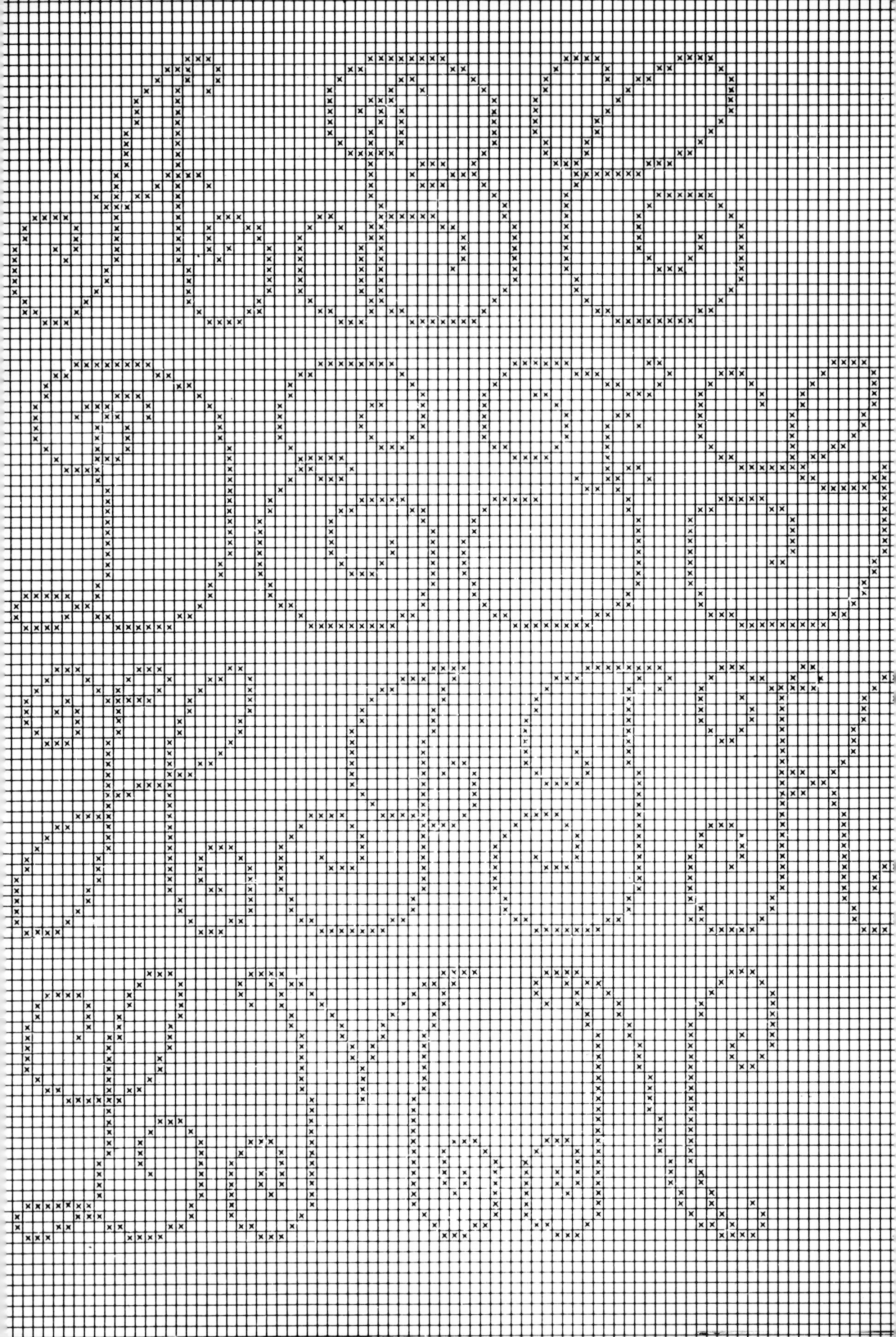

Alphabet

The alphabet is used as the basis for many embroidered samplers. A chart is given here for all the letters from A to Z. Each cross represents one embroidery stitch.

Appliqué picture

This cotton appliqué picture combines
the arts of appliqué and embroidery.
The embroidery is used to emphasize
the contours of the design. It also
adds richness of colour and texture.

Looking after work

Antique embroidery. This can so easily disintegrate, and special care is recommended. You can sprinkle dry powder, such as french chalk or potato flour, over the embroidery and then brush it off gently.

Cleaning embroidery. Test the colour-fastness of threads and fabric first by dabbing work on the wrong side with dampened cotton wool. If it proves to be colour-fast, wash in a mild detergent and tepid water, gently easing the water through the unfolded fabric by laying it flat and pressing it with the palm of your hand. Rinse the work until the water is crystal clear, then roll it in a towel to remove excess moisture. Lay the embroidery out flat in an airy passage (or use a hair drier) until damp dry, then iron it on the wrong side, over a soft, padded surface, and leave to air thoroughly.

Dry cleaning. This should only be used on professional advice as the various dyes in the embroidery could be damaged by the cleaning fluids.

Pressing embroidery. Never press work on the right side. Place work right side down on a soft, padded surface so that the stitching will not be flattened. Press on the wrong side with hot iron over damp cloth.

Removing dust. Suspend the needlework out of doors and beat it gently on the wrong side with a wooden spatula. To remove damp dust from colour-fast items, immerse the needlework in a bath of tepid water, keeping it outstretched throughout and changing the water until it remains clear. Remove the moisture by rolling the needlework in towels and dry it away from direct heat.

Reviving colour. Add a tablespoon of white vinegar to the rinsing water to heighten colours.

Stains. Try to remove these as soon as possible. Place the needlework over absorbent paper and dab it with cotton wool and white spirit; then rinse thoroughly. Strong chemicals and bleaches should not be used. Grease can generally be removed by rubbing in talcum powder and leaving it for a while before brushing out gently. Warm milk will remove ink stains and methylated spirits will remove ballpoint-pen marks, but both must be rinsed in tepid water afterwards to avoid ring marks.

Storing needlework. Make sure it is mothproofed (with crystals from chemists). If possible, roll the needlework around a cardboard cylinder to prevent creases, which weaken the materials. Store in plastic bags or in dark tissue paper in an atmosphere that is neither too dry nor too damp – say 60 to 70 per cent humidity.

Bookmark

This is worked in cross-stitch on evenweave linen with fringed ends. A chart for the bookmark is given below. Repeat in reverse from the centre to complete the design.

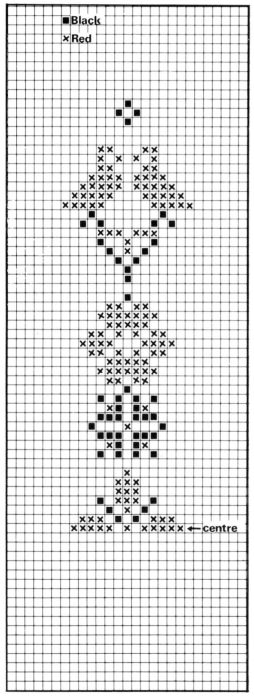

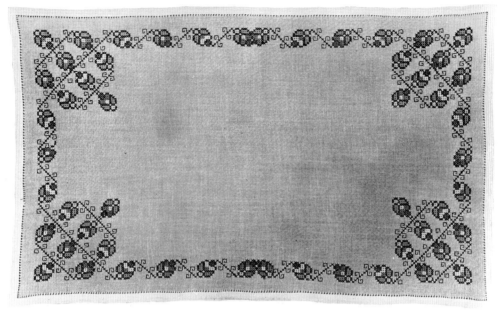

Yugoslavian embroidery

Work this traditional design in cross stitch and running stitch, following the pattern from the chart. Each stitch must be worked over the same number of threads in each direction. Mark the centre of the fabric before you begin. Complete the pattern in reverse direction from the centre.

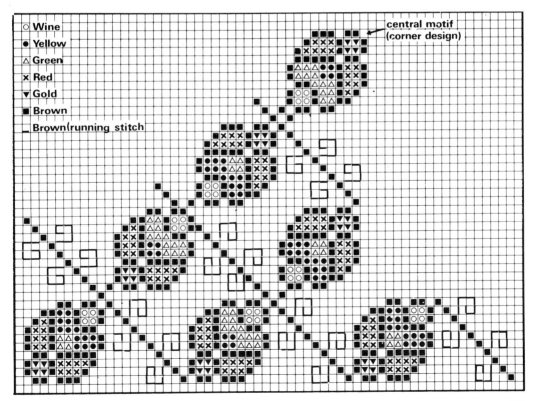

○ Wine
● Yellow
△ Green
✕ Red
▼ Gold
■ Brown
— Brown(running stitch)

central motif
(corner design)

PATCHWORK

Equipment

Fabrics. The easiest fabrics to use are those that do not stretch or fray and which fold easily. Cottons, man-made fibres, silks and velvets will all do, providing they are non-stretch, non-fray and easy to fold.

It is best not to mix fabrics of different weights in the same piece of work, as obviously a heavy damask will drag down a fragile patch of cambric next to it. When mixing old and new, wash both – the new to prevent any shrinking, the old to make sure that it will take to water, unless the thing you are making is a decorative object that will not need washing.

Templates. In early patchwork the shapes were made without templates, those precise master-shapes from which the papers could be cut accurately into the shape required; materials were just cut and folded by hand. But quilting patterns needed templates to ensure the accurate repetition of an outline. Many templates were made by the men of the family, from a variety of materials, usually oak, tin or card, with others in silver, brass, copper, pewter and occasionally ivory and bone.

Templates can still be made at home in the larger shapes; but as accuracy is so very important in the small shapes it is best to buy the commercial variety in metal or hard plastic. These are available in most of the traditional geometric shapes in a variety of sizes.

There are pairs of templates for each given shape and size, a 'solid' and a 'window'. The solid represents the size of the finished patch, and so becomes the pattern from which the paper linings are cut; the window is for marking out the actual patches on the fabric.

Needles. These should be as fine as the materials you are using, and sizes between 8 and 10 are best. Either 'sharps' or 'betweens' can be used; a 'crewel' needle, with a long eye, in size 9 or 10, is obviously easier to thread.

Pins. Fine and smooth ones should be the rule, to avoid marking the fabrics. Dressmaker's pins, brass lace-pins, and the very short, fine pins – 'lills' or 'lillikens' – are just right for tiny patches.

Scissors. These should be moderate in size and weight, but sharp and with good points. You need two pairs – one for cutting the fabric patches, and one for cutting the paper patches. Alternatively, you can use a craft knife for cutting the papers.

Thread. Cotton is suitable for most fabrics, but you need silk thread to work on silk. The cotton should be fine, 60, 80 or 100, and you can use it on linen, satin and velvet. When joining a light and a dark patch, the stitches will show less if you use a dark thread.

Paper. The paper linings must be firm and crisp to achieve well-shaped patches and can be cut from good-quality scrap paper or card. (Bank statements, company reports, if not too shiny, Christmas cards, and cartridge paper are suitable.) You can buy ready-cut papers in various sizes too; the most important thing is that all the patterns for one piece of work should be cut from paper of the same thickness, otherwise the patches will not be identical. Iron-on Vilene is also suitable instead of paper where the material needs to be stiffened.

Miscellaneous. You will also need a sharp lead 'B' (medium-soft) pencil, for marking out patches on the wrong side of the material. Use a white dressmaker's pencil if you have to mark on the right side of fabric. (Never use an indelible pencil or ball-point pen as they will mark the fabric.) A sharp razor blade or seam ripper is useful for any unpicking.

The collection of cushions below show some of the many forms patchwork can take.

Method

Making the patches. The basic method is to cut out the fabric either by laying a paper on the material and cutting a suitable amount of turning beyond it, usually about 1cm ($\frac{1}{4}$in) on normal fabric and a medium-sized patch; or by laying a template on, drawing round it (a coloured pencil is usually easier for the drawing) and then cutting along the pencil line.

The paper is put on the wrong side of the fabric and folded firmly over the material along one side, close against the edge of the paper. Using pale tacking cotton and a fine needle, the turning is tacked down with one stitch.

The next side is folded and tacked, pinching the turnings firmly into place at the corners. Continue all round the patch. To make sure it is folded accurately and with no gap left between paper and folded edge, another paper is laid on top of the patch, and if a very small amount sticks out evenly all round, the patch has been tacked accurately.

Joining the patches. Two patches are laid together with the right sides facing, and the papers outward, and fine oversewing stitches made along one side. The same depth of stitch should be maintained all the time and the stitches should be firm and fairly close, avoiding the paper. When the two patches are joined, the seam is opened and pressed flat, on the wrong side. It doesn't matter if the stitches are not wholly invisible, they are not meant to be – this is characteristic of patchwork.

It is best to sew patches into convenient groups or units, and for the units to be sewn together to complete the finished article.

Finishing off. When the whole area of patchwork has been sewn, all the tacking stitches are taken out, and the work pressed well on the right side according to the type of fabric. The papers come out last.

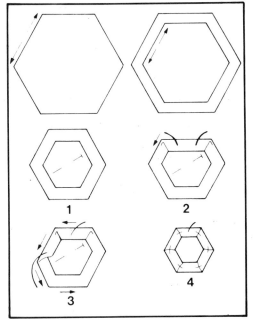

A hexagon template (top), and how to use it (centre and below).

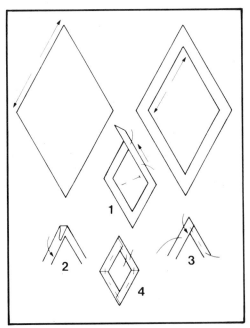

A diamond template (top) and how to use it (centre and below).

Patchwork shapes

There is no standard size for patchwork shapes: they can be as large or as small as the patchwork item requires.

The six-sided hexagon, or honeycomb, is the easiest shape to construct, and can be arranged in a number of ways to create interesting mosaic patterns.

The diamond is slightly more difficult to work than the hexagon because of its two sharp points and needs great care in construction to achieve well-shaped patches. The broad angles are worked in the same way as in the hexagon, but the sharp points need a double fold as shown. Diamonds can be used to make up other shapes such as the star, box, trellis and cube. The elongated diamond can also be used in much the same way.

Squares. Quilts made from squares alone are rare. Squares can be effectively combined with hexagons, triangles and diamonds. Accurate cutting of templates is particularly important with squares to ensure that corners fit.

The triangle can be made, either by dividing a diamond shape in half horizontally, or by dividing a square diagonally.

The clamshell patch is obviously based on the segment of a shell and its other names, shell, scallop and scale, are all appropriate because the scalloped lines usually overlap each other like the scales on a fish.
The usual method of construction is that an unlined patch is made by turning down the semi-circular edge only. This is done by fine pleating to make an accurate shape, following the outline of a card reproduction of the solid template which has been pinned into the right side of the patch.

The log cabin is an evocative shape; narrow pieces of varying lengths are laid end to end representing the over-lapping logs in the cabins of the early settlers. No template is necessary for log cabin as the patches are measured strips of material which are sorted into light and dark shades, with the strips worked into a square. The overall design depends on the relationship of light and dark strips and there are several variations on the traditional log cabin arrangement, of which 'barn-raising' and 'straight furrow' are the most well known and evocative.

The Log Cabin Cushion (left) is so called because its light and dark shades look like overlapping logs. Below are examples of crazy patchwork.

Crazy. A random effect can be obtained by sewing together patches of different sizes and uneven shapes in a crazy paving fashion. This is known as crazy patchwork. It is great fun to do, and very easy. The kaleidoscope effect was particularly popular with the Victorians. Shakespeare's wife, Anne Hathaway, had a crazy patchwork coverlet on her bed at Stratford-upon-Avon which can still be seen there today.

A rose-garland design made up of hexagons.

Floral patches form a variety of patterns on a plain background.

Planning the design

Planning falls into two main sections: colour and geometric shape, and use of the finished patches. In most cases one must look at the colour first by seeing what material is available, and then one can decide on the size and shapes of templates that should be used to give a proportionate pattern in relation to the size of the article being made.

It is important to remember that the more sides a template has the bigger the area covered by it, in relationship to the 'edge' size. So for a cushion, a hexagon of up to 2.5cm (1in) would be large enough; in the case of a diamond on its own you could comfortably use a 3.5cm (1½in), and if one were using an octagon for a cushion, 2cm (¾in) would be big enough.

Having decided the size and shape of your templates it is best to draw out your design on a piece of graph paper; and then using a very sharp pencil draw round your templates.

A simple way to design is to arrange tacked, ready-to-sew patches on a cork mat or polystyrene (expanded foam) tile, playing around with them until a pattern emerges, formed by the different tones and colours. Then fix each patch to the background with a pin, removing the patches one at a time. To make sure that they are sewn together in the right order, make a rough drawing of the patches, marking the centre of each one with the appropriate colour.

A piece of printed fabric can be the starting point of a design; for instance, a small flower-patterned fabric with tiny roseheads, could have the flowers cut out and centred in the patches and alternated with plain ones, the patches having, preferably, a background colour in common.

Nineteenth century box and diamond quilt of silk, satin and velvet.

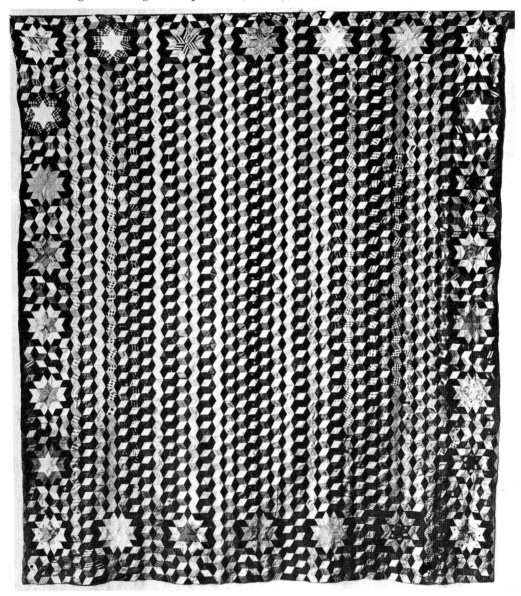

Tulip quilt of
percale appliqué on light wool.

Applied patchwork

It is thought that the crusaders going to Palestine in the eleventh century brought patchwork home to England in the form of gay banners. For centuries it was highly thought of at Court, and during the reign of Henry VIII fine specimens of combined embroidery and patchwork were made. It was really patch upon patch because before the motifs were applied to the foundation, they were elaborately embroidered in intricate designs; and even after that the edges were enriched with gold and silver cord. Thus applied work is where patches are sewn to the surface of the material so that they form a pattern either by their own shape and colour, or by the shape and colour of the ground materials.

Sewing patches onto a fabric ground appliqué or in applied fashion can contribute to really creative patchwork. Many of the applied patterns in traditional patchwork were cut from partly worn fabrics and stitched onto a new foundation in order to preserve them. Flower, figure and bird motifs were cut from printed cotton chintzes, which lend themselves to extremely interesting designs being formed.

The large quilt opposite incorporates both commercial patterns and home-made motifs.

A nineteenth century dressing gown made of silk and chiné hexagons.

Fashion

Accuracy and neatness are particularly important when making clothes in patchwork. Patches must be accurately cut and properly tacked on to the papers. The stitches must be small and taken right into the corners. Fastening on and off must be very secure.

If you just want to bring a touch of fashion to small articles, try trimming an apron in patchwork circles at the waist and hem, and a sleeveless plain blouse at neck and waist. These patchwork touches will brighten the dullest garments.

It is a good idea to buy a simple pattern of the dress, skirt or trousers of which you like the styles, lay it out on a table and see what size and shapes of patches would be most convenient to use. You may find that by interlocking the patches you can do away with some seams. Some experts recommend poplin as the most suitable material for a beginner to use as it does not fray so much.

*Right: a Victorian
parasol rejuvenated
with a bright diamond
patchwork covering.*

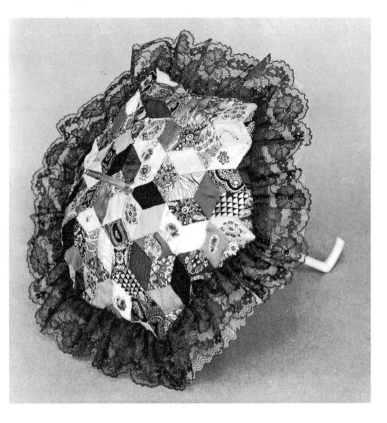

*The apron and blouse
(below) are brightened
with patchwork circles
and hexagons.*

Rocking-horse coverlet

This rocking-horse coverlet is a lovely present and can be made very quickly for the nursery, using a sewing machine and omitting the templates. The measurements in the coverlet illustrated are 80 × 140cm (32 × 56in) but they can easily be adapted.

Materials

2.25m (2½yd) gingham
25cm (¼yd) navy, 20cm (⅜yd) white and 50cm (½yd) red – all patterned fabrics
22cm (9in) square plain red fabric for horse
Centre piece 51cm (20½in) square
Lining and interlining.

Method

Trace the rocking horse; enlarge to 30cm (12in) in length. (Alternatively, trace any farmyard animal from a child's drawing book or nursery frieze to use in the centre.)
Cut out sections, allowing 5mm (¼in) turnings, and slip-stitch in position, inserting a little wadding in the horse's mane, saddle and tail. Use knots of stranded cotton around the saddle. Add the 10cm (4in) squares (allowing 5mm or ¼in for seam turnings) all round the centre piece as shown.
Cut the gingham, lining and interlining to measure 85 × 145cm (34 × 58in).
Assemble the whole on a flat surface and then sew through all three layers of squares diagonally and vertically. Work two rows of stitching, 5mm (¼in) apart, around centre motif to keep the layers of material together. Finally, add a 2.5cm (1in) border all round, allowing 5mm (¼in) for turnings on each edge.

CANVAS WORK

Equipment

Canvas. This is available in a variety of widths and thicknesses. Single-thread canvas is available in sizes of 10 to 40 threads to 2.5cm or 1in.

Double-threaded canvas is available in sizes of 5 to 24 pairs of threads to 2.5cm or 1in.

Needles. These should have blunt points and the size selected should slide through the canvas without forcing its threads apart.

Threads. These must be of good quality, suitable for hard wear.
Tapestry wool is available in a wide range of colours and some shades are available by weight for backgrounds. If crewel wool is used it can be stranded for the thickness required for the size of canvas.

Frames. Use a strong, square upright frame to keep the canvas taut and the stitches even throughout. The size of the canvas should not exceed the length of the webbing attached to the rollers of the frame. Fold the canvas over before sewing it firmly to the webbing. Selvedges should be laced to the sides of the frame.

Charts. Work one stitch for each square on a chart in the colour indicated in the key.

Stitches. Keep all the stitches slanting in the same direction unless otherwise stated.

Stitches

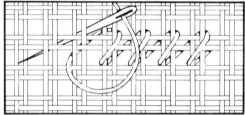

Gros-point. This is worked on double-thread canvas, from right to left. Take the needle over one crossing of double threads on the front of the work and under two crossings of threads to bring it into position for the next stitch. Reverse the position of the needle for the return rows as shown for petit-point.

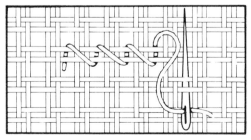

Half-cross-stitch. Work from left to right – inserting the needle one

36

thread up and one thread to the right and bringing it out one thread down to the end of row. Work the return row from right to left, inserting the needle one thread down and one thread to the left and bringing it out one thread up – to end.

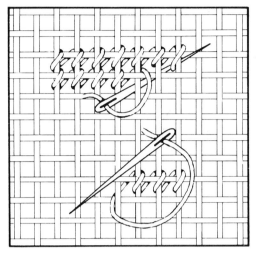

Petit-point. This is worked on single-thread canvas, from right to left. Take the needle over one crossing of canvas threads on the front of the work and under two crossings of threads to bring it into position for the next stitch.

Reverse the position of the needle for the return rows from left to right.

Method

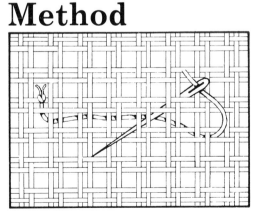

To begin. Make a knot at the end of the wool and insert the needle through the threads a few squares away from the first stitch. Work the first couple of stitches over the thread

lying at the back of the work, then cut off the knot and continue stitching. To end off the wool, run the needle through the last few stitches worked, on the wrong side of the work.

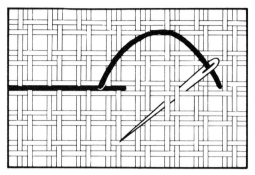

Trammé. Bring the thread out at the left-hand side of the canvas, carry it along the required distance and re-insert the needle through the canvas. Bring the needle out through the laid stitch and continue laying the thread for the distance required. This thread helps to cover the canvas threads completely and adds extra wear.

Blocking. The character of the stitches is inclined to pull the work to one side. To rectify this requires a little time and patience. Place the work, right side down, over squared paper on a flat board. Stretch it back into shape, pinning it securely about every few centimetres (inches). Cover the back of the work with damp blotting paper or a damp cloth and leave under a weight until completely dry. It may be necessary to repeat this process to get the work absolutely square and ready for mounting.

Mounting. It is possible to get this done professionally at art needlework shops. Furniture can also be made to fit embroidery, and vice versa. If the mounting is done at home, use a strong linen thread to lace ends together in each direction as shown in the diagram.

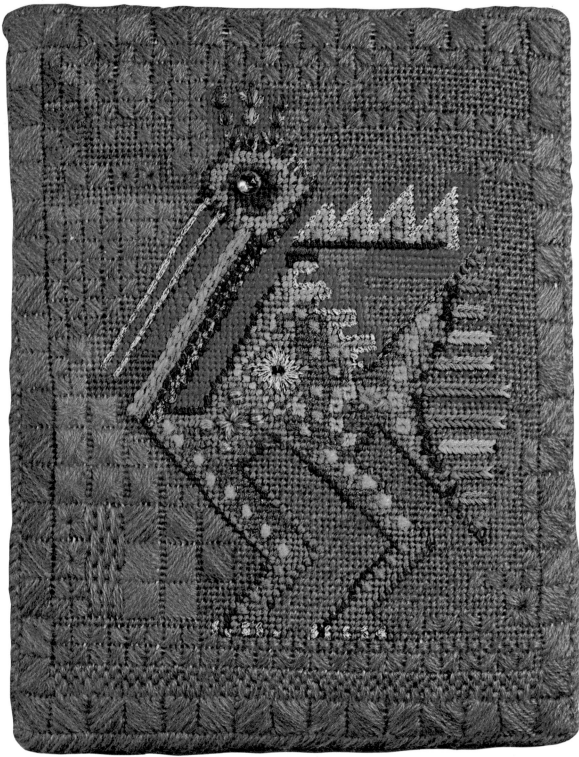

*Imaginative use of stitches gives
an exciting texture to this exotic panel.
The background is of different
shades of orange.*

Bird

This exotic bird displays an imaginative use of canvas stitches which create an exciting texture for this panel. Metallic threads highlight the bird and the use of different shades of tan makes a lively background. Besides the petit-point and couching, the following stitches were used:

Double-cross-stitch (a) Work cross-stitch over four threads as shown and bring the needle out four threads down and two threads to the left. (b) Insert the needle four threads up and bring it out two threads to the left and two threads down as shown. (c) Insert the needle four threads to the right to complete the stitch.

Fern-stitch. Bring the needle out at arrow. Insert the needle one thread down and three threads to the right; bring it out two threads to the left. Insert the needle one thread up and three threads to the right; bring the needle out four threads to the left in readiness for the next stitch.

Parisian stitch. Work straight-stitches over two and four canvas threads alternately, interlocking successive rows as shown.

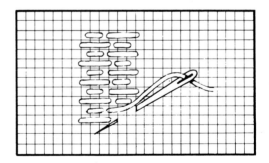

Star-stitch. This consists of eight straight-stitches worked over two canvas threads through the same centre hole as shown.

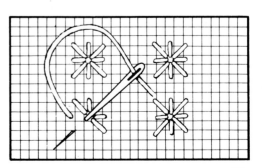

*An interesting application
of various canvas-work stitches.*

Bevy of butterflies

These butterflies were all worked in separate squares and sewn together afterwards with linen thread. Assembled squares is a pretty idea for adapting any small motif that would be insignificant alone yet forms a strikingly effective design. Each square should measure about 10cm (4in) for a medium-sized cushion. For the back of the cover use a square of toning needlecord. The colours shown here can be easily varied. The individual squares are easy to carry around and work on in odd moments. The embroidery is done in half-cross-stitch throughout and may be highlighted with gold thread couching for an exotic effect.

41

*A colourful sample showing
bargello-type patterns on single
thread canvas.*

General hints

1. Working thread must cover the canvas completely.

2. Keep stitches even and sloping in the same direction throughout, unless patterns are designed to alternate.

3. Use short lengths of thread, say 45-50cm (18-20in) for working.

4. Buy all background wool of the same dye lot.

5. 25gr (1oz) of tapestry wool works approximately 20sq cm (8sq in) of gros-point.

6. Keep selvedges at each side of the work.

7. For hard wear, lay thread between canvas threads and cover with stitching.

8. When you have completed a few stitches, let the needle and thread dangle to untwist itself.

9. Allow good margins around the work for mounting.

10. For a first exercise choose something small – it will be completed more easily and more ambitious pieces can be undertaken later. Small items are also easier to keep clean.

CANDLE MAKING

Equipment

Strictly speaking, a candle is a piece of wax with a wick embedded in it. Therefore, strictly speaking, one could take a block of paraffin, insert a wick, and call the resulting object a candle. Touch a match to the wick and the thing would burn as a candle is supposed to burn. However, even the most undemanding critic would not be impressed by such a candle, and inserting a wick into paraffin would satisfy no one's creative urge. If you plan to make candles at all, you owe it to yourself to use the same fine materials that professionals enjoy. Good candlemaking supplies are not very costly, and the results can more than justify the expenditure of a few pounds at your nearby hobby shop.

Wax, wicking, and mould. To begin with, provide yourself with a good grade of paraffin and a few metres (yards) of wicking.

The easiest candle for the novice to make is the poured candle, and for this you will need a mould. Almost anything that can hold melted wax until it hardens can serve as a mould, but for the best results you should have at least one finely crafted metal candle mould. These come complete with wick holders, with gaskets or screws for sealing wick holes, and with directions for wicking. If it is cared for properly, a good metal mould will last for ever.

If you wish to begin with one mould, a one litre (2pt) square or round metal mould is most satisfactory for first experiments in candlemaking.

Stearin. In addition to wax, wick, and mould, you must have stearin. This substance, derived from fats such as tallow and butterfat, is sold in the form of powdery, white crystals. It is added to melted paraffin to make a finished candle more opaque. Stearin also raises the melting point of paraffin, so that candles do not sag or bend in a warm room. It makes white candles white and coloured candles bright.

Dyes. Special candle dyes should always be used for coloured candles. These are available in several forms: cakes of intensely coloured wax from which small chips can be shaved, granules of wax, liquids, and tablets.

Mould release. Nearly every candlemaker uses a mould release of one type or another. The release is applied to the inside of the mould before the candle is poured, just as butter or margarine is rubbed around the inside of a cake pan before the cake batter is poured. After the candle has hardened in the mould, it will slide out more easily if mould release has been used.

Salad oil makes a fairly satisfactory mould release if it is applied sparingly. Hobby shops offer fine silicone sprays especially for candlemaking. When using mould release, it is important not to be too enthusiastic. If you apply too much, droplets may form inside the mould and the finished candle will have little bubbles in the surface. If you use salad oil, wipe the inside of the mould with a tissue before pouring the candle to be sure that you have removed any excess which might mar the candle.

Perfumes. Perfumes are not absolutely necessary in a candle, but they supply a nice finishing touch. Candle perfumes come in a wide variety, ranging from the familiar bayberry and rose to exotic fragrances like patchouli and frangipani.
Follow the manufacturer's directions. If you don't have directions, use discretion. A few drops to each kilogram of wax should be enough.

Containers. It is safest to use a double boiler to melt wax over boiling water. If you don't have a double boiler, you can construct one. Put a trivet in the bottom of a large pan. Pour water into the pan, and then put the pot in which you will melt your wax on the trivet.
You probably already have a suitable water-bath container. This is any vessel, such as a plastic or metal wastepaper basket or a large bucket, which can be partly filled with water. After you have poured hot wax into a mould, you hasten the hardening of the wax by putting the mould into the water bath.
Some moulds tend to float when put into a water bath, so keep a heavy object on hand in case you have to weigh the mould down. Clean bricks or large trivets make fine weights for moulds.
You can, if you wish, pour wax directly from a double boiler or melting pot into a mould, but it is neater and safer to use a container with a handle and a pouring lip. A 1 litre (2pt) pyrex measuring jug makes a

Basic equipment including wax, wicking, stearin, mould, mould release, dyes, melting pot and sugar thermometer.

perfect pouring container. A kettle with a pouring spout is also fine, although not as easy to keep clean.

A sugar thermometer is essential. It is necessary to know the temperature of the melted wax at all times, and there is only one way to do this. Clip a sugar thermometer to the edge of the melting pot or double boiler and watch the temperature.

A skewer or ice-pick is very useful for chipping wax into small chunks for faster melting. As a candle hardens, a skewer can also be inserted into the centre to see if the wax has contracted and pulled away from the wick, leaving a cavity that must be filled. In addition, a skewer can be heated and used as a wick rod to make wick holes in candles which have been moulded without wicks. (If you do not have a skewer or ice-pick, try using a small screwdriver.)

Basic safety

Melt wax over boiling water. Water cannot get hotter than 100°C. Wax will not vaporize and ignite at this temperature so the candlemaker who uses a double boiler should not have any difficulties.

Never leave melting wax unattended. Even if you are going to step out of the room for only a second, remove the wax from the stove or turn off the burner under the wax.

Always use a sugar thermometer. It is not necessary to bring wax even to 100°C for candlemaking. Watch the thermometer and remove the wax from the heat when it reaches 93°C.

Keep working areas away from the stove. Newspapers covering work surfaces could catch fire.

Use pot holders or oven gloves when handling melting pots or pouring containers. Use only pouring containers with handles or pouring lips or spouts.

Never dip a candle into boiling water.

If the wax catches fire, turn off the heat and put a lid on the pot to smother the flames.
Keep an open box of baking soda ready. If wax spills onto the stove it will almost certainly burn.
Turn off the stove and throw handfuls of baking soda onto the burning wax. Never use water to try to put out a wax fire.

If you should spill hot wax on your hands – or any other part of your anatomy – do not try to wipe it off. Run cold water over the wax. It will harden instantly and can be lifted off. Treat the burn at once.

*Candles have great decorative potential; they can be made in
household objects, unmoulded or left in the containers, or cast
in sand or foil, decorated with wax chunks or colourfully
stacked.*

Method

Melting the wax. Put water in the bottom of your double boiler, put wax chunks in the top and place over the heat. As the wax begins to melt, slip the sugar thermometer onto the edge of the double boiler or the melting pot so you can keep track of the temperature of the wax at all times.

Preparing the mould. First, spray the inside of the mould with release and insert a wick into the mould. All commercial moulds come with instructions for wicking, and these should be read carefully.

Water bath. Now put cool – not cold – water in the water-bath container.

Wax. When the wax reaches a temperature of about 82–88°C (179–190°F), add stearin – 54ml (3tbsp) to a 0.5kg (1lb) of wax for a white candle, and 36ml (2tbsp) for a coloured one. Stir in the stearin and add dye, a tiny bit at a time. When the dye is completely dispersed through the melted wax, test for colour either by dropping the wax onto a white surface or by putting some wax into a cup of water. When your wax reaches 93°C (199°F), remove it from the heat immediately.

Pouring. You are now ready to pour the candle. (If adding perfume, now is the time.) Pour away from the stove. Reserve a small amount of wax in the melting pot – a half to one cup will be sufficient – and put the melting pot back on the heated water. Use oven gloves or pot holders to hold the warm mould and the pouring container. Tilt the mould slightly and pour melted wax down the side of the mould to prevent air bubbles from forming. Fill the mould to within a couple of centimetres of the top, or until you have a candle as tall or short as you desire – considering the size of the mould, of course.

The water bath. After pouring the wax into the mould, set the mould in the water bath to harden. The water in the water-bath container should be deep enough to reach almost to the top of the mould, but not so deep that water will run over into the mould. Weight the mould down if necessary.

Topping up. After the candle has cooled in the water bath for about half an hour, reheat the wax you have reserved in the melting pot. You will see that a skin has formed on top of the candle. Insert an ice-pick or skewer into the candle next to the wick two or three times to break this skin and relieve the surface tension of the wax. A cavity in the candle, called a well area, will be apparent. This is caused by the contraction of the wax as it cools. Fill this cavity with the wax you have reserved. Wait another half hour and again use the ice-pick or skewer to test for cavities. If any appear, refill the well areas. After 30 minutes more, test again for cavities and refill any well areas. After two or three hours, remove the mould from the water bath. Let the candle continue to cool inside the mould for another six to eight hours.

Finishing. Finish the candle by trimming the extra wick from top and bottom. It is unlikely that the bottom of the candle will be absolutely even. Correct this by using a cheese grater to trim off excess wax, then smoothing the bottom of the candle by rubbing it gently on a heated frying pan. If the surface of the candle has been marred by handling, rub away the imperfections with an old nylon stocking.

1. *Before using mould, coat it with mould release or salad oil.*

2. *Insert wick into mould and through retainer screw, if any.*

3. *Fasten wick to wick holder, making sure it is in centre of mould.*

4. *Keep an eye, meanwhile, on the thermometer in the wax.*

5. *When melted wax has reached the right temperature, add stearin.*

6. *Add dye in tiny quantities and test for finished colour.*

7. *When wax reaches 93°C remove it from heat or turn off burner. Add perfume if desired.*

8. *Wipe melting pot to prevent drops of water falling into the wax. Pour away from stove.*

9. *Use an oven mitt when pouring warm wax. To avoid air bubbles, tilt the mould.*

*A vast range, both of bright primary colours
and subtle muted shades can be obtained.*

Colour

Candle dyes are pure pigment suspended either in wax or in oil. They are so concentrated that a red dye can appear almost black and a bright yellow may look like a very deep brown.

Unless you plan to go into candle-making on a truly enormous scale, do not attempt to bypass the craft shops and mix your own dyes.

Use the dyes which are sold especially for candles. The range of colours available is enormous. You can purchase deep red, hot pink, orange, yellow, lavender, purple, bright blue, brown, black, and almost any shade

in between these colours.

Mixing colours. If you wish, you can start out with the three primary colours: red, yellow, and blue, and blend your own shades.

If you find the dyes too brilliant add a bit of black.

Do not be hasty when putting dye into melted wax. The dye is extremely strong, and a tiny bit at a time should be added. It is easy to put dye into wax, but it is impossible to get it out again once it's there, so proceed with care.

Testing for colour. The colour of the melted wax in the double boiler or melting pot will not be the true colour of the finished candle. As the wax sets in the mould and becomes solid and opaque, the dye colour will become deeper and richer.

The intensity of the finished colour is determined by the amount of dye used and do bear in mind that a little goes a long way. Test for colour by dropping some dyed, melted wax into a cup of water or onto a saucer. The wax will harden to an approximation of the final colour.

A novice candlemaker can start with as few as three colours. But remember the colour wheel (above) and blend primary colours as desired. Combine yellow and blue to get green – light green or dark green, depending on the proportion of yellow to blue; blue and red for purple; red mixed with yellow for orange. Add a bit of black to make brilliant colours more muted. For pink, add a minute amount of red dye and use more stearin.

Improvised moulds

Pyrex baking dishes and custard moulds can be first-class moulds. They are heat-resistant and inexpensive, and they come in a number of sizes.

Ordinary glassware can also be used to mould candles. For a pleasing, cone-shaped candle, try pouring wax into a lager or beer glass.

Bear one thing in mind when selecting moulds from the cupboard. You want to get your candle out of the glass – or fancy mould – once the wax has hardened. Containers which are wider at the top than at the bottom, such as lager glasses and fancy moulds are easier when it comes to unmoulding. Containers with straight sides can be used, however. Coat the container with mould release before pouring wax. If the candle does not release after it has hardened, you need not give up and throw away the glass. Put it into hot water until the wax has softened, then turn the container upside down and let the wax slide out. Clean the glass as you would any candlemaking utensil – by putting it into a warm (not hot) oven, and then washing it.

Wicking after unmoulding. You will probably mould candles in bun trays, glasses, and pyrex dishes without wicks. Wicks can be inserted after a candle is unmoulded. Use a wire-core wick. Dip it into warm wax and pull it taut. Then, with a heated skewer, make a wick hole in your candle. Insert the wire-core wick into this hole and seal by pouring a tiny bit of warm wax around the wick. Cardboard containers or tin cans can be wicked before a candle is poured or after is has been moulded.

Pouring temperatures

Metal and glass moulds. Pouring temperatures for metal containers should be the same as for professional metal moulds – 82–93°C (179–199°F). If you use glass, let the wax cool at

Almost any food container can be a mould.

Transfer wax from utensils to foil in warm oven.

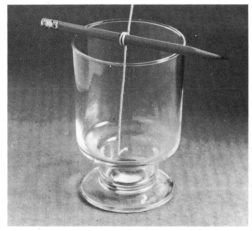

Suspend wick in glass before filling.

Some more ideas for candle moulds.

least to 77°C (170°F) before pouring, and warm the glass first by putting it into the oven and setting the heat at low – very low. Leave the oven door open so that the glass does not overheat and shatter.

Cardboard and plastic moulds.
When using cardboard moulds, let the melted wax cool almost to 63°C (145°F) – or until it has a skin on the top – before you pour. If the wax is too hot, it may burst through the container, causing some damage.

Plastic containers can be slightly more heat-resistant than cardboard, but do not count on it. Cool the melted wax at least to 66°C (150°F) before pouring into plastic. Pour a small bit at first, to see how the plastic stands up. If it holds its shape, fine. Go ahead and fill the container. If it doesn't hold its shape, you have lost nothing but one disposable container, and you haven't spilled hot wax all over the kitchen counter.

Layered candles

Making a layered candle is one way to use leftover wax. Two different colours of wax are adequate. Three colours are more fun, and you can use as many as four or five. Suit yourself about colour combinations. A layered candle can be as muted or as mad as you please.

You must have more than one pouring container for a layered candle, since you must keep several batches of dyed wax molten at the same time. The pouring containers must have handles and pouring lips. Several of the smaller pyrex measuring cups or aluminium measuring jugs will do.

Heat about 1kg (2lb) of medium-temperature paraffin wax in the top of a double boiler. Use a sugar thermometer. When the wax reaches 82°C (179°F), add stearin. When it reaches 93°C (199°F), remove the double boiler from the heat, wipe the bottom of the melting pot dry with paper towels, and divide the melted wax by pouring it into two, three, or more small pouring containers.

Add dyes to the liquid wax in the pouring containers, and test for colour as described earlier.

Keep the wax warm and molten by putting the pouring containers on trivets which have been placed in a pan of hot water. Almost everyone has a big, flat-bottomed roasting pan which can be used in this way.

Bring the water in the pan to a boil, then turn the heat down so that the water just simmers. It isn't practical to clip a sugar thermometer to the rim of each pouring container, but if you use trivets and keep the water in the pan just under the boiling point, the wax in the containers will remain liquid and it will not overheat.

If you are using leftover wax, you can disregard the double boiler. Put chunks of dyed wax into the pouring containers and place these on the trivets in the pan of hot water. The wax will melt. And if you have an electric frying pan, you will not even need trivets.

Electric pans have automatic temperature controls. Put the pouring containers into the pan, fill the pan with water, set the temperature control at 93°C (199°F) and do not worry. The warm water surrounding the pouring containers will keep the wax at an even temperature, and with that automatic control nothing can get too hot.

Horizontal stripes. When pouring wax in layers, do not tilt the mould but pour carefully and directly into the bottom of it. Try not to splash wax on the wall of the mould.

Wicks and wick holders can get in the

For diagonal stripes, tilt mould.

An unusual layered candle made in a cream carton.

*Doubly attractive in being both pretty
and economical, layered candles are a useful
way of disposing of left over wax.*

way of a good, clean pour, so pour into a wickless mould. If there is a hole in the bottom of the mould, seal it with masking tape or mould sealer. After pouring the first layer of coloured wax, let it set and harden a bit. For a clear-cut line of separation between colours, the first layer of wax should be quite firm before the second layer is poured. For a gentler blending of colour, the second layer can be poured while the first layer is still warm. Test the hardness of the first layer of wax by prodding it in the centre with a pencil or the handle of a wooden spoon. The wax should be slightly tacky even if you want a sharp separation between your coloured layers. It can be almost liquid if you want the colours to blend into one another.

A candle poured in layers will contract and sag in the middle just as surely as any other candle. Do not let this worry you. Save some wax when you pour the last layer. After the candle has set and the depression appears in the centre of this last layer, use your reserved wax to fill the depression and even off the top.

Water baths are not usually used for layered candles. Let the candle remain in the mould overnight, to make sure it is completely cold, then unmould it.

Wicking. Add a wick, using a hot skewer to make a wick hole. A wire-core wick will insert most easily. The size depends on the size of the layered candle.

Diagonal stripes. You get diagonal stripes by tilting the mould.

Rest one side of the mould on a support. A medium-thick paperback book or a little stack of magazines will do.

Pour a layer of colour into the mould and let the wax set. Then pour a second layer of colour and let that set. If you're working with a third or fourth colour, pour those layers. When the first three or four layers are firm, turn your mould and tilt it in the opposite direction, using the paperback book or stack of magazines to keep it steady.

Pour several layers of colour, letting each set between pourings.

Tilt the mould again, if you wish. When the layered wax has nearly reached the top of the mould, set the mould level. The last pouring should be all one colour, and it must be poured when the mould is on the level. Reserve a little wax to fill any depression which may appear in the top of the candle.

The diagonally striped candle is unmoulded and wicked just as the regular candle is unmoulded and wicked. Make sure it has completely hardened before you remove it from the mould.

Note that it is not wise to pour half of a layered candle one day and the second half another day. Once the layers of wax you poured on the first day cool and harden completely, they may not be receptive to the layers of wax you pour on the second day. Cold wax is brittle, and it tries not to adhere to warm wax. If you start to pour wax in layers, finish in one grand operation – or you may have a candle which will do its best to break in half. You may also ruin the layered surface. Cold wax can pull away from the walls of the mould, and warm wax added to layers of cold wax can seep down between the cold wax and the mould and spoil the design of the candle. It can also bind the candle into the mould.

Chunk candles

To make a chunk candle, you need all your regular candlemaking supplies and you also need chunks of coloured wax.

If you have leftover wax, you may already have chunks. If you don't have leftover wax, you can make chunks and have the advantage of being able to plan the colours.

Making chunks. Heat medium-temperature paraffin wax in a melting pot or double boiler. Use a sugar thermometer. When the wax reaches 82°C (179°F), stir in stearin. Add dye and test for colour.

Coat a flat-bottomed container with mould release. Candlemakers sometimes suggest using a baking sheet for chunks, but baking sheets are large. Unless you want heaps of chunks, a square sandwich tin is satisfactory.

Pour the hot, dyed wax into the sandwich tin. How much you pour depends on how thick you want your chunks to be. You can pour 1cm ($\frac{1}{2}$in) of wax, 2cm ($\frac{3}{4}$in), or even more. For free-form chunks, your task is simple. Let the wax in the tin get completely cold, then turn it out and break it up with a hammer.

For chunks that are more restrained – small squares or strips of wax – you will have to cut them. Do not let the wax in the tin get cold and hard. Let it solidify, but start cutting chunks while the wax is still warm and malleable. Use a paring knife to cut the warm wax, and work from the outer edge of the tin towards the centre, since the wax in the centre will not harden as quickly as the wax round the edges.

If you find that you have miscalculated, and the wax in the pan is too brittle to cut, you can start again. Remelt the wax, pour it into the tin, and again wait for it to set.

After you have cut all the wax in the tin into chunks, let the chunks get thoroughly hard, then turn the tin upside down. The chunks will drop out.

Once you have chunks, you can proceed to make a chunk candle.

With one or two exceptions, chunk candles are made exactly the way all moulded candles are made. Prepare your work area and wick your mould in the usual manner.

Melt medium-temperature paraffin wax in a melting pot or double boiler, using a sugar thermometer.

Do not add stearin.

If you use dye – and you probably will, since undyed wax looks grey – use it sparingly and choose a colour that will complement your chunks – light yellow for orange chunks, or pale pink for bright pink chunks.

Pouring. When the wax in the melting pot is ready – that is, when dye has been added and the wax is at about 82°C (179°F) – put a handful of chunks into the mould. Pour liquid wax over these. Chunk candles are usually poured a little at a time, and about 2.5cm (1in) is as much as you should attempt on the first pour.

Omit the water bath. Let the wax set around the chunks in the mould. Prod between the chunks with your skewer and fill any air cavities that appear.

When the first pouring has set, add more chunks and more wax. Let the second pouring harden and fill air cavities. Then add more chunks and more wax. Repeat until you have filled your mould or run out of chunks or liquid wax.

Let the candle remain in the mould overnight, then unmould and finish it as you would any other candle – trimming excess wax off the bottom with a cheese grater and rubbing the bottom on a hot frying pan to smooth it. Cut off extra wick.

Chunk candles; another decorative means of using up wax.

Variations. The chunk candle can be varied in several ways. For example, chunks made without stearin will melt more quickly than chunks containing stearin, and the candle-maker can use them for a marbled effect. You can put them in a mould and pour on very hot wax, so that the chunks blend and run together, colouring the candle from within. The smaller the chunks, the more easily they will melt and blend and provide a subtle final effect.

If you want to avoid marbling, add extra stearin to the wax you will use for chunks. When the chunks have set and are in the mould, do not cover them with very hot wax. Let the liquid wax cool to 75°C (167°F) or less. If the chunks are not sufficiently visible inside the finished candle, you can remove some of the wax from the surface of the candle by dipping the candle into hot water. Remember to allow for displacement. Use hot, but not boiling, water and be sure you have plenty of extra wick protruding from the candle. The best and safest way to dip a candle is to hold it by the wick.

Cut chunks as thick or thin as you wish from a sandwich tin as the molten wax begins to harden. Work from outer edge of pan towards centre where the wax will remain liquid longest.

Start with a first layer of a couple of centimetres, putting chunks in mould a handful at a time. Chunks need not be accurately placed in mould.

Pour hot, dyed wax over chunks, being careful to avoid air cavities. Let the wax set. Then repeat until candle has reached the desired size.

Flower candles

Candles with flowers embedded in them are made in two parts. There is a centre candle – a core candle – and an outer shell of wax which contains the floral decorations.

To make a flower candle, you need all the usual candlemaking supplies. a core candle, a fairly large-diameter mould, and some flowers and leaves. The core candle must be about 2.5cm (1in) less in diameter than the mould for the flower candle.
Pin dried or plastic flowers and leaves to the core candle.

Wicking. Insert the core candle into the mould, wick first. Thread the wick through the wick hole in the bottom of the mould and secure it by sealing the hole with masking tape.
Melt paraffin wax and add dye that will blend with the colour of your inner core candle.

Pouring. Pour wax into the space between the core candle and the wall of the mould. Pouring temperature should be about 82°C (179°F). A water bath is not necessary. Watch the wax set, prod around the core candle with your skewer and fill any well areas that appear.
When the candle is cold, unmould it. If you want your flower candle to have an 'exfoliated' look – that is, if you want the surface of the flowers to extend beyond the surface of the candle – melt away some of the wax shell surrounding the core candle by rolling in hot, but not boiling water.

Basic equipment for flower candle.

Prepared core candle in mould.

To show up well, flowers must touch walls of the mould.

ORIGAMI

Origami is the craft of paper folding and was invented over a thousand years ago by the Japanese.

Basic method and symbols

The basic symbols of origami are given here. These indicate the types of folds which are standard in origami and, with practice, they will become readily understandable. Their application is illustrated in the charts opposite.

A
1   valley fold   -------------------------
2   peak fold   - · - · - · - · - · - · -
3   cut off   -------------------------➤✂

The first two symbols, which are shown above (A) are the most indispensable and basic of all origami chart symbols. In folding it is possible to do one of two things: fold the paper forward or fold it away from the body. Actually performing the processes indicated in chart A results in a piece of folded paper that looks like the one in chart B.

B
4   fold forward
5   fold under

The arrows (B) are intended to prevent mistakes and valley folding where you should peak fold, or vice versa. Do not confuse these arrows

with the ones in C which describe the technique used. This symbol

C
6   stairstep fold   ⚡

indicates the kind of fold used in making birds' beaks or the shells of shrimp, etc. It is no more, actually, than a valley fold and a peak fold used together. (See Chart C)

D
7   hidden line or the outline of a part's former position   ····················

Sometimes explanatory charts will begin where the square of paper has already been folded once, as in D. The symbol in 7 is then used to indicate the shape and position of the paper before that fold. The same symbol is used when the process illustrated by the line passes under or between two layers of the paper as in chart D.

I   pocket fold
II   hood fold

The folds I and II shown in charts D and E are so basic that there would be no origami without them. Because the hood fold (II) is a little hard to follow in chart D, chart E has been added to make it easier. Both D and E result in the hood fold shown in step 3. You should become sufficiently proficient with these folds to make a hood fold together with other folds as series D shows. A more detailed explanation of I and II follows in the illustrations overleaf.

E
8   pull
9   hold this place down
    with your finger ○

You will understand symbols 8 and
9 if you study E1, 2, and 3.

F
10   turn the figure over

This symbol means you are to turn
the entire figure over.

G
III drawn inward   IV drawn outward

Though the processes in chart G
are easy with practice, at first they
seem difficult. They must be learned,
however, since they are often used.
Folding in step 1 then opening out
again in step 2 is simply for the sake
of making creases needed later in
the process.

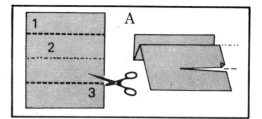

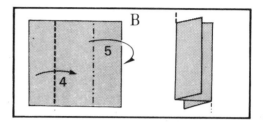

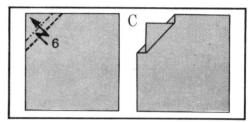

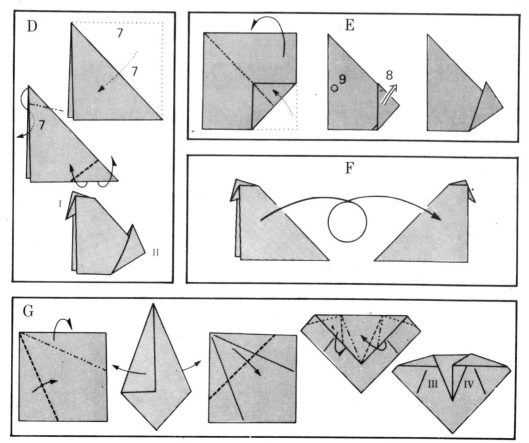

Look fairly closely at the hood and the pocket folds. If you make a sharp point 2, the most important feature in the general effect of origami, you will see that you have one side (A) that is closed, and one side (B) that is open. If you fold the point toward side A, you will get a hood fold. If you fold it toward side B, you will get a pocket fold. Do not mistake the hood and pocket folds for mere valley or peak folds, or you will end up with the wrong folds like those in 3'.

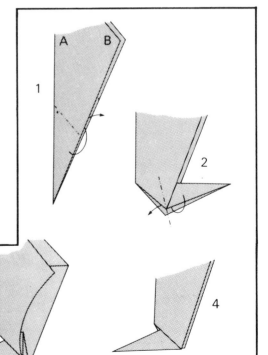

Folding propping parts

When making the feet of birds and animals, if you fold the point in the direction of side A and end up with a hood fold in accordance with the theory just explained, you will get something that is poorly closed and balanced. Folding it toward side B, however, gives a good prop. Adjust it so that it looks like 4.

A hen

Aside from some with unusual shapes, all bird folds begin with Basic Fold IV. For this reason, Basic Fold IV is called the Bird Base. It is described on page 68. But to make the hen shown on the previous page it is necessary to begin with the very first step in the Bird Base. The head section (10) will turn up again. Although it seems difficult at first, mastering it is important.

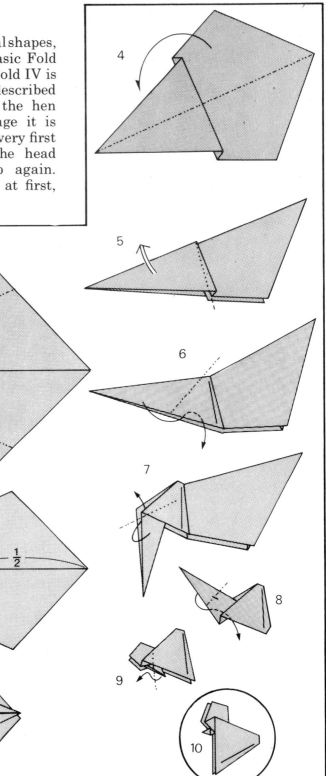

A flying eagle

Step 11 is the most difficult. Bring points A and B to the positions shown in step 12, and the rest of the folds will fall into place.

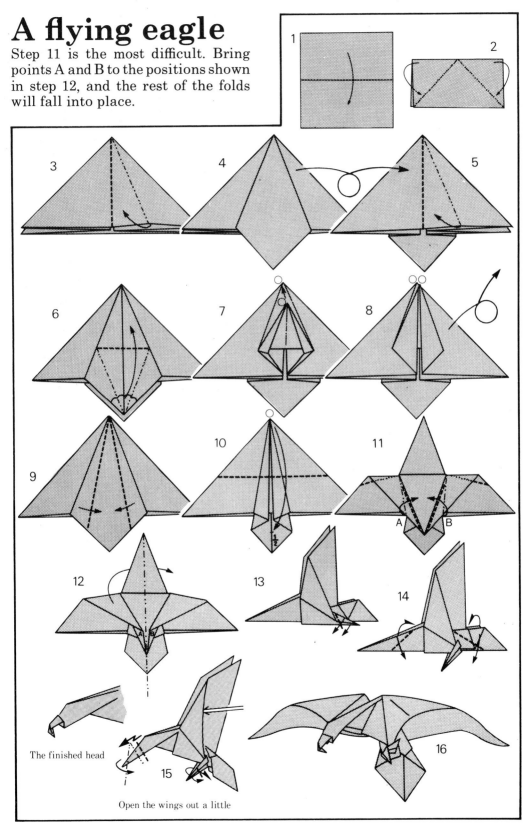

The finished head

15

Open the wings out a little

The bird base

These diagrams show how to fold the Bird Base, or Basic Fold IV. Since all of the rest of the birds in this chapter use this base, fold a number of them now for practice. The crane, the classical masterpiece of traditional Japanese origami, is folded from this base. All of the following folds will begin with step 10, be sure you have ends A and B pointed in the right directions each time.

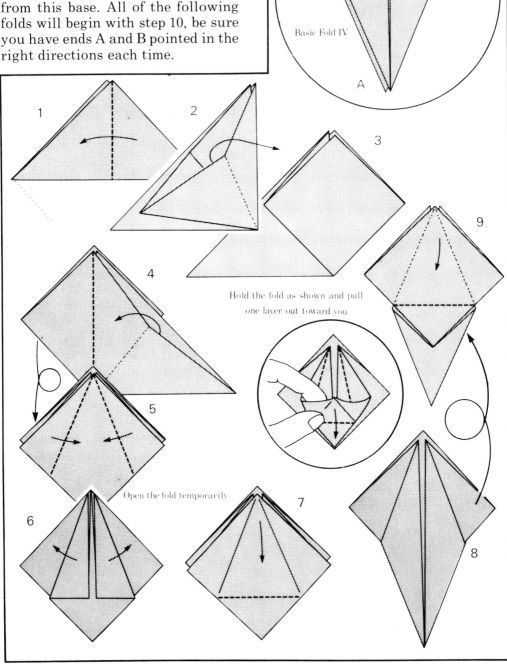

Basic Fold IV

Hold the fold as shown and pull one layer out toward you

Open the fold temporarily

Crane and flamingo

The big difference between the origami crane and flamingo lies in the way the beaks are folded and in the colour of the plumage. Actually, the folding of the body in both birds is practically identical. Prepare a sheet of white paper and a sheet of pink, and fold the two at the same time. When you get to the beak section, you can make one of each.

Eliminate the steps for shortening the tail in steps 4 through 6, and fold it so that it looks like the picture. (The flamingo pattern is overleaf.)

Begin with Basic Fold IV

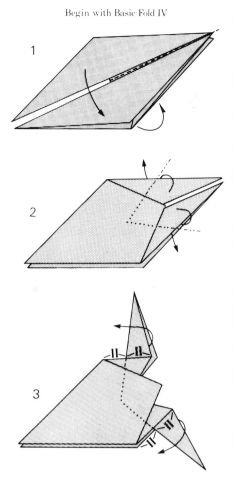

1

2

3

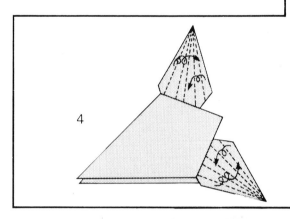

4

Peacock

Since in the crane and flamingo the two legs are folded from the very middle of the Basic Fold, the birds are quantitatively equal in the head and tail halves. If the legs are brought closer to the neck, the tail section inevitably grows longer. This simple idea gave rise to the peacock fold.

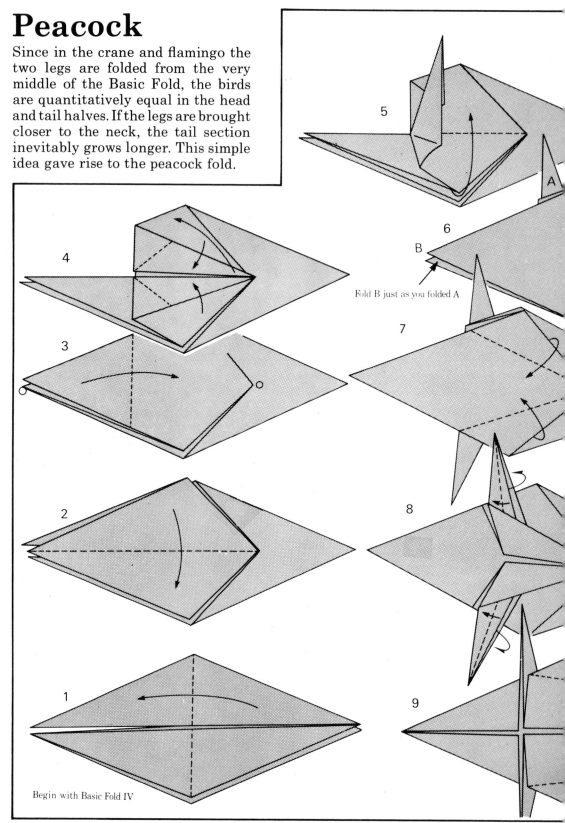

5

6

B

A

Fold B just as you folded A

7

4

3

8

2

9

1

Begin with Basic Fold IV

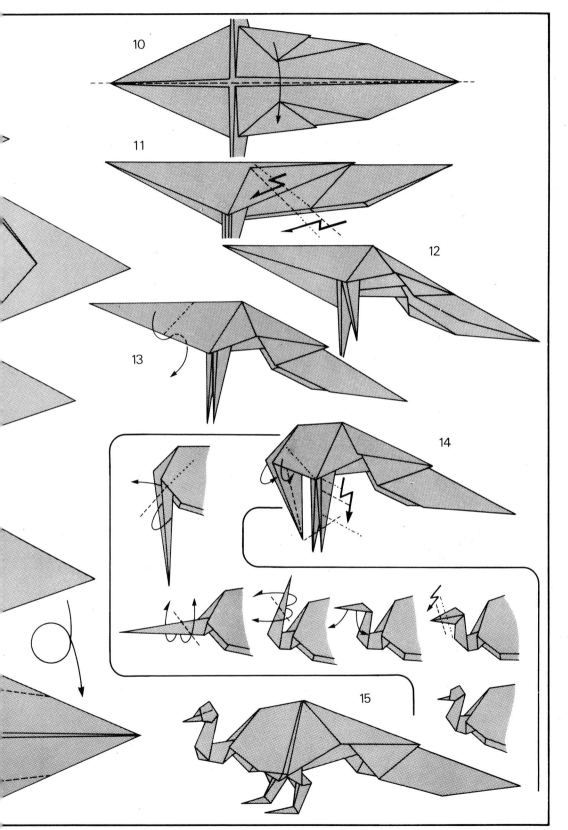

10

11

12

13

14

15

Lady of fashion

Fold the arms out about one quarter of the way down the height of the figure.

By adjusting the positions of the arms you can alter the expression. Make a crease at the spot where widths a and b are the same and fold in numerical order.

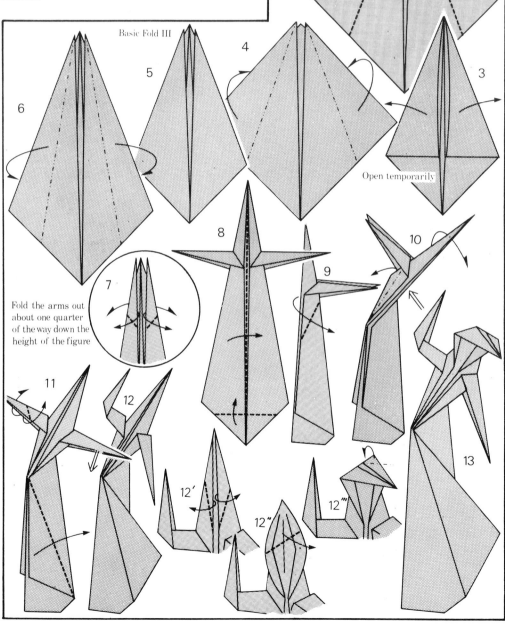

Basic Fold III

Open temporarily

Fold the arms out about one quarter of the way down the height of the figure

Giraffe

The task of folding this giraffe is made simpler by giving it three, instead of four, legs. Some of the giraffes in the photograph were made by cutting the single rear leg along the middle to make two rear legs.

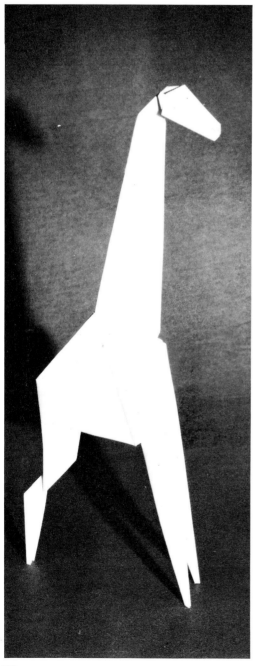

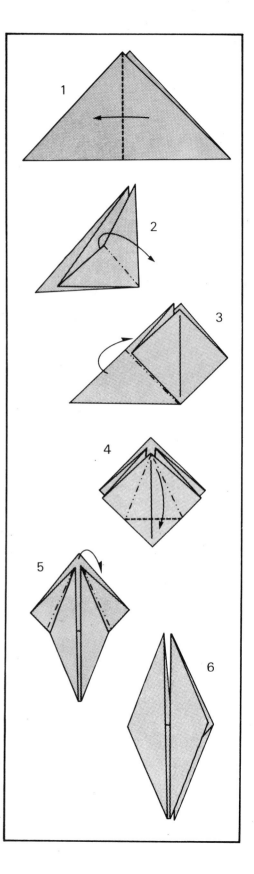

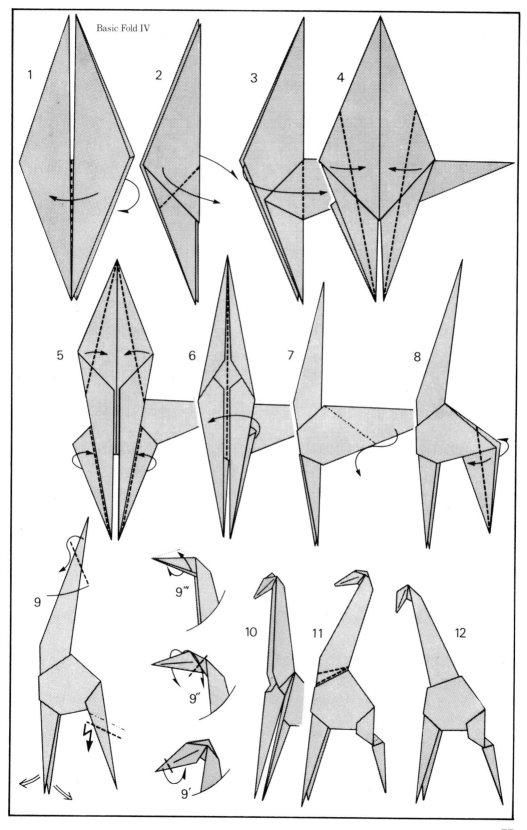

Basic Fold IV

1

2

3

4

5

6

7

8

9

9'''

9''

9'

10

11

12

SOFT TOYS

Grid system

The pattern for each toy in this chapter is on a grid. Each square on this grid represents 2.5cm (1in). To transfer the pattern, draw a grid of 2.5cm (1in) squares. On this grid mark with dots where the lines of the drawing cross the lines of the grid. There are two sizes of grid used in this chapter. The very small squares will have to be multiplied by 4, and the larger squares multiplied by 2 to bring them up to 2.5cm (1in). You can, of course, make the toys larger than their intended size by drawing out your own grid of, say, 5cm (2in) squares.

Useful equipment

1. Sharp cutting-out scissors.
2. Scissors for cutting paper and card.
3. Small, very sharply pointed scissors.
4. A selection of needles.
5. Wire nippers.
6. Stuffing sticks – a blunted pencil, blunted wooden skewer, blunted orange stick, blunted cocktail stick.
7. Very sharp pencils, black and white, or white tailor's chalk.
8. Felt-tip pens – black, red, brown, blue.
9. Transparent thread, tape measure.
10. Ruler, compasses.
11. Masking tape.
12. Colourless upholstery adhesive.

13. Thin card, tracing paper.

Dolls

It is a very interesting hobby to make a collection of dolls, and then to dress them in the national costume of different countries.

Because felt does not fray, it needs no turnings; but if you make your doll in fabric, then you must allow 1.25cm ($\frac{1}{2}$in) extra for turnings.

Felt Dolls

Felt dolls are easy to make because felt is so easy to work with.

It is easy for children to use for dressing their dolls too – the colours are gay and very varied and when the dolls are small it is the most successful means of dressing them.

Be careful when pinning felt because pale colours do mark easily, and always pin as near to the edge as possible so that any marks will be hidden by the sewing.

When leaving unfinished work, always stick the needle in on the edge or in some stitching or embroidery already done.

When transferring designs for embroidering to felt, trace the design on to thin paper, place this in position for the embroidery and work running stitch in contrasting cotton through paper and felt, afterwards

Felt dolls are very easy to make and fun to dress.

tearing away the paper. The stitching or embroidery will hide the running stitches, if they cannot be pulled out. When tracing round templates, as for instance, for a doll, use a sharply pointed pencil and do not press down too heavily. You may find that the resulting outline is a smudgy thick line, so always trace on the wrong side of the material, and cut out the shape, if possible, inside the traced lines; otherwise seams may appear grubby and soiled.

Most of the dolls are sewn together on the right side, either with over-sewing or stab-stitch, which in appearance is rather like running stitch (see page 11). In this way, both edges of material are kept together, one not moving more than the other.

Materials
Felt.
Some soft stuffing material like kapok.
Embroidery silks.
Wool or silk for making hair.
Material for dressing.

Method
There are two ways of sewing up felt dolls, either by oversewing or by stab-stitch, as has been stated.

If you are going to oversew, then trace round the template (Fig 1) twice and cut out the pieces, cutting just inside the pencil lines.

Pin the two pieces together, matching the heads, hands and feet, and then oversew, starting from the top of a leg, round the legs, arms and head, leaving one side open for stuffing.

If using stab-stitch, fold the felt in half and trace one outline onto the doubled material. Tack round the outside of the shape (Fig 2), and stab-stitch it together, leaving one side open for stuffing. When finished, trim

off the surplus felt as close as possible to the stitching.

Legs. Stuff the legs first, pushing the stuffing gently into the felt with a blunted pencil or orange stick. Stuff thinly near the tops of the legs if you are going to make a jointed leg so that the doll can sit. To do this, sew a row of close stab-stitch or back-stitch across the tops of the legs (Fig 3).

Head and arms. Stuff the head and arms, keeping the parts flat rather than round, or the stitches may pull. Take care, too, not to pull too hard on the corners of the opening or the felt may tear. Stuff the rest of the body and sew up the opening.

Features. Embroider the features with embroidery silks; felt-tip pens are not very successful on felt, because the hairy surface makes the outline smudgy.

Hair. Hair can be made in several ways – for straight hair, or plaits, cut lengths of wool to reach from shoulder to shoulder over the head (Fig 4). Spread them out over the back of the head and catch them down the centre with back-stitch, like a parting. Bunch them together at the side and tie with bows, or plait the ends. Curls can be made by threading a darning needle with brown or yellow wool; take a stitch through the head on a previously marked hair line across the forehead, place a finger on the strand of wool close to the head and wind it two or three times round the finger. Slip the loops off and catch them down on the head with a couple of stitches through all the loops. Repeat this, sewing the loops close together all along the hairline, then filling in the rest of the head (Fig 5). Separate the loops by ruffling them with your hand.

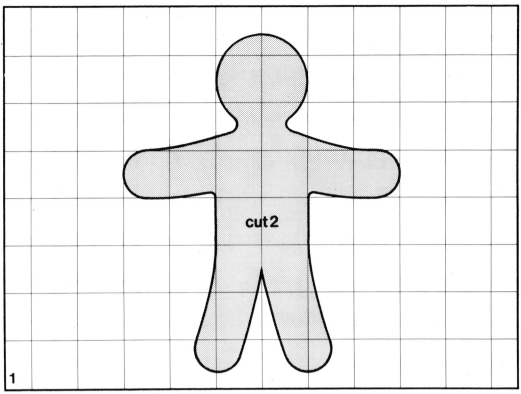

Each square on the graph equals 2.5cm (1in). Enlarge and transfer the design.

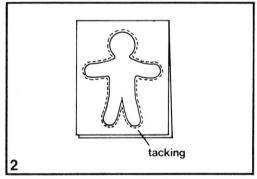

Tack round outline of the shape.

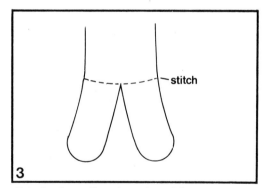

Stitch along line for jointed leg.

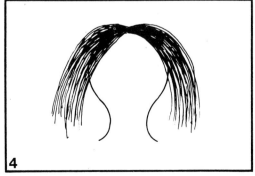

Straight hair can be made from wool.

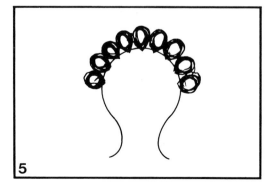

Curly hair can be made too.

Animal toys

If you doodle when you are thinking, you will know how the doodles take all kinds of fantastic and imaginative shapes. Some of the toys here are like that because they can be evolved from many different shapes – circles, squares, ovals – placed together in various ways, to achieve an animal shape, or something recognizable.

A cat from circles

Materials
Felt.
Embroidery silks.
Kapok.
Cotton for sewing.
Ribbon.
Card.

Method
Draw a 15cm (6in) circle for the body with a 10cm (4in) circle above it and overlapping it to form a head and neck.

On the smaller circle draw two triangles with curved sides for ears, and extend the curve at the base of the large circle to make a curled tail (Fig 1). This shape when cut out will be your template.

Trace round it twice, reversing the template the second time to keep the pencil marks all on the one side (Fig 2).

Oversew the two pieces together, leaving an opening at the base. Fill it smoothly with small pieces of kapok, pushing it gently into the corners of ears and tail, not too hard – it should be flat rather than fat.

Sew up the opening.

Cut a shield shape in black felt for a nose and sew in position.

Embroider two curves for the mouth in stem or chain-stitch and straight stitches in black silk for whiskers (Fig 3).

Cut two ovals with pointed ends, and two black centres, for eyes, and sew them in position on the face, slanting in towards the nose.

Finally, tie a bright ribbon or felt bow round its neck.

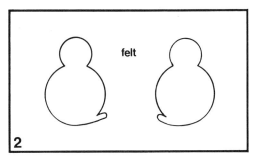

Two circles form the body and head.

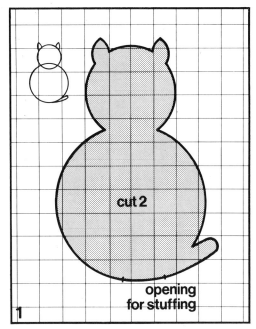

Cut out two outlines with template.

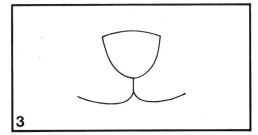

Embroider mouth in black silk.

A rabbit from ovals

Materials
Felt.
Kapok.
Card.
Sewing cotton.

Method
Draw a large and a small oval over-lapping at the ends. Add a smaller oval at the opposite end of the large oval for a tail, add two long oval ears, and an oval front paw.
Cut out this shape in the card and trace round it on to the piece of felt. Cut two shapes in felt, pin them and sew them together, leaving an opening in the base. Then push small pieces of kapok carefully into ears, tail and front paw. Stuff the head, then the body. Sew up the opening. Cut out felt eyes, following Fig. 1, and glue in place.

Ovals form the rabbit outline.

Work a nose and mouth in single chain-stitch (Fig 2) and three or four straight stitches each side for whiskers.

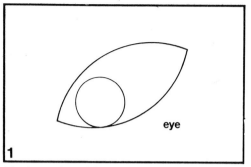

Each eye is a felt oval and circle.

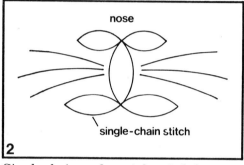

Single chain and straight stitch for nose and whiskers.

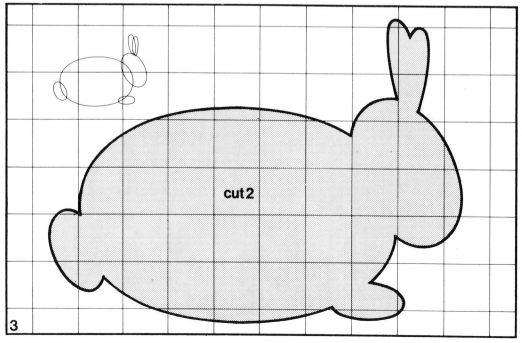

Slither toys

These toys, shown overleaf, are made from two pieces of material filled either with soft stuffing like kapok or foam chippings for a soft cuddly toy, or partly filled with rice or lentils for a slithery toy which can be used for throwing like a ball – it is much easier to catch because it is not a hard shape – or for sliding across a shiny surface.

Any fairly solid-looking round or square shape is suitable. The slither toy, whether it is a round, fat bird, a sitting cat, a duck, frog, fish or tortoise, should be unfussy with no hanging pieces.

A slither tortoise

Materials

Two pieces of felt about 30cm by 23cm (12in by 9in) to make a toy 23cm (9in) long, or two pieces in different colours for top and bottom (choose a fairly dark colour for the underside), or any strong cotton material.
A card template.
Embroidery silks.
Sewing cotton.
Rice or lentils.

Method

Draw an oval of the size you want your tortoise to be and add a blunt head, a pointed tail and four short legs (Fig 1).

Trace round this on to the felt or material. If you choose felt, cut round the pencil line, but if cotton material is used, cut round 1cm ($\frac{1}{2}$in) outside the line to allow for turnings.

Draw a wavy line all round, just inside the edge of the piece. This will be the top of the tortoise (Fig 2). Criss-cross inside it with wavy lines to indicate the pattern on the shell.

Embroider on the lines and round the edge in stem-stitch or whipped running-stitch. Place the pieces together with the right sides outside and pin them together at the head, tail and legs. Oversew the edges with matching cotton, leaving the tail end open. Pour in spoonfuls of rice until it is about a third or less full – if you have made a large size then pour in less than this proportion, or the finished toy will be much too heavy. Sew up the opening.

If you are using cotton material, embroider the top piece on the side, which is not pencilled, taking care to keep the pattern inside the allowance for turnings. Pin the two pieces together at head, tail and legs with right side inside. Machine or backstitch all round the pencil line, leaving the tail end open. Trim off some of the turning allowance, cut out little 'V's on the curves to allow the seams to lie flat and not pucker. Turn it inside out and press the seams flat.

Pour in the filling, turn in the seam allowance at the tail-end opening and oversew firmly.

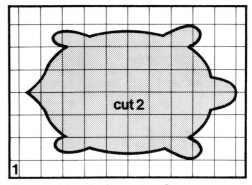

Cut two identical tortoise shapes.

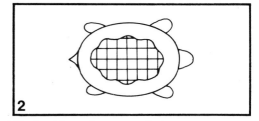

Embroider criss-cross design.

85

A slither fish

Materials

Two pieces of felt 30cm by 24cm (12in by 9½in) to make a 26cm (10in) fish, or two pieces of different colour.
Rice or lentils for filling.
Embroidery silks.
Matching sewing cotton.

Method

Trace round the template (Fig 3) on the felt and cut out two pieces. If using material not felt be careful to leave about 1cm (½in) allowance for turnings. This will not be so easy to sew at the tail because of the narrow base, so use felt if possible.

On the piece for the top embroider little crescents in chain-stitch to resemble scales and a wavy line all round from the head, along the base of the fins and the base of the tail (Fig 2). See chapter one for embroidery stitch technique. Sew on a

circle of white felt, or embroider a big eye (Fig 1).

Pin the two sides together with right sides outside and pin at the mouth, fins and tail. Oversew the edges all round, leaving the tail end open.

Pour in rice or chosen filling, not more than a third full, and oversew the tail edges. Sew right through the base of the tail so rice cannot get in.

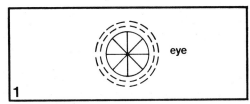

Embroider a big eye.

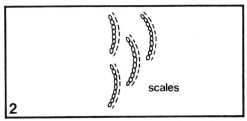

Chain stitch the fish scales.

Each template square equals 2.5cm (1in).

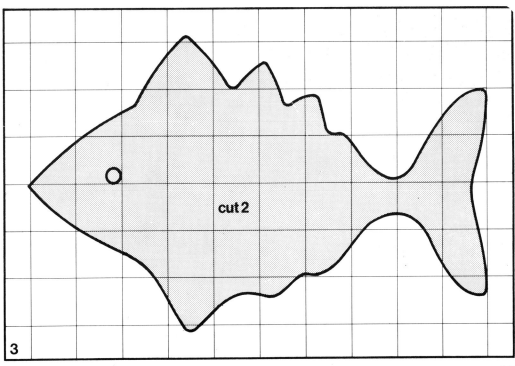

cut 2

A slither frog

Materials

Two pieces of felt 26cm by 30cm (12in by 19in) to make a 28cm (11in) frog.
Contrasting felt for spots.
Rice or lentils for filling.
Embroidery silks.

Cut out two pieces from the template (Fig 1) and embroider one piece for the top with big eyes, or sew on circles of felt, and some coloured spots on his back. Pin the two sides together with wrong sides facing and oversew all round, leaving the tail open. Sew across the base of each leg to prevent the filling getting in, because the weight of it can weaken the felt across the narrow base and in the toes. Fill to much less than a third and sew up the opening.

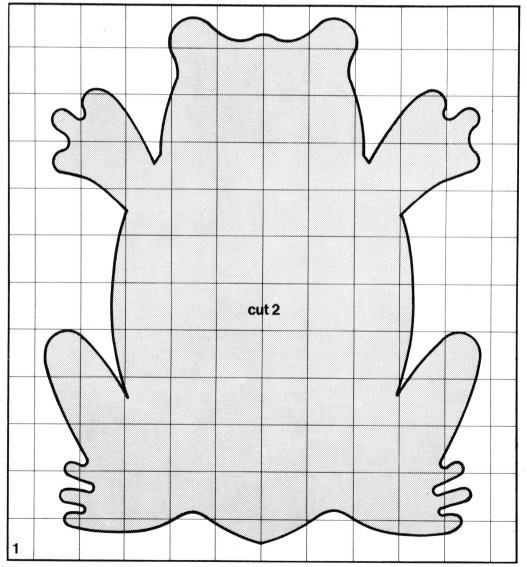

cut 2

1

Sew across narrow base of each leg to prevent filling getting in.

A dog

Materials
Felt.
Stuffing.
Embroidery silk.
Sewing cotton.

Method
Cut out two pieces of felt, following the template enlarged from Fig. 1. Embroider an eye on each piece.

Pin the pieces together at nose, ears tail and feet. Oversew the edges, starting at the inner edge of front leg (Fig. 2) and sewing round it and on over the head to back of the neck. Stop here and stuff head and front leg with small pieces of stuffing, pushing it gently into the corners and seams of foot and head. Continue sewing over the back and the back leg. Sew half of inner leg seam and then stuff the back foot. Sew rest of leg. Stuff leg and body. Sew underbody seam.

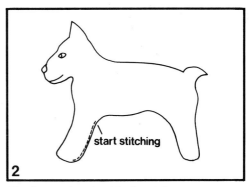

Begin sewing inside front leg.

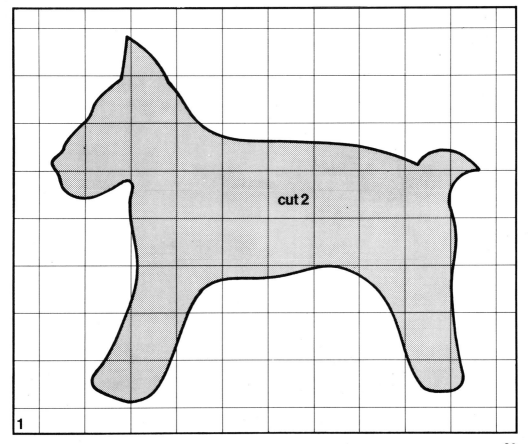

POTTERY

Clay is one of the oldest of all craft mediums and dates back to pre-historic cultures. Originally forms were built up free-hand or on a simple mould and dried in the sun. A variety of outer coatings were added. With the discovery of fire, it was found that by placing clay vessels on a bed of coals, they became capable of withstanding heat. The potter's wheel and the kiln were subsequent technical improvements.

Slab

A slab of clay is exactly what the term implies, a ball or hunk of clay rolled out to an even thickness with a large dowel or rolling pin, and the rough edges trimmed off. Much of the contemporary pottery in shops and exhibitions is, in fact, made from slabs joined together, and this forming technique, along with coil-building, is the basis of the projects. In working with the slab method you will find that it lends itself not only to geometric shapes but also to more spontaneous ones, such as the vase below. This pot was made of six slabs - two for the bottom half, two for the upper section, and two for the handles.

Coil

The technique of coiling goes back in time as far as pottery itself and is the process which eventually led to the wheel method. With the hands, clay is rolled into long coils which are joined and circled round and round to build a vessel or other form. Below is a large coil jar about 915mm (3ft) high which was formed in little less than an hour. A beginner at pottery could work just as quickly but the scale of work undertaken is bound to be limited by the size of kiln available.

Coiling is a most satisfying method for beginners because it allows the formation of the pot to be fully appreciated and controlled.

Slab pot with natural flowing lines.

Coil pot of a more classical shape.

Combining slab and coil

The two major approaches to hand-built pottery, slab and coil, can be combined. A good example is the pot shown. The body is slab-built, and the decoration pieces of coil and stamping.

Besides using 'found objects', conventional pottery tools and the hands to texture a surface, simple stamps of your own design can be used to pattern the damp clay. This type of decorative device dates back to pre-Christian times, and originally was probably a way of signing pots. Many modern potters use stamps as a form of seal or signature.

Egyptian paste

Egyptian paste is a kind of clay that duplicates closely the material from which the ancients made their ceramic beads. Jewellery can also be made with regular clay, but this must be dried, then bisque-fired, glazed, strung on nichrome wire, and fired again.

Egyptian paste clay needs only to be shaped and fired. The materials can be purchased from any pottery supplier. Egyptian paste can be handled in the same fashion as regular clay: it can be rolled, made into slabs, patted, pinched, or any of the other various forming methods from which beads can be cut or otherwise made.

Pot constructed of slabs and coils.

Collar of unglazed Egyptian paste.

Texture

When the basic form of a pot has been made, there are two ways of decorating or finishing it. The surface of the clay can be textured, or the entire pot, or parts of it, can be glazed. Texturing is a blanket term for the processes that give variation to the clay surface; some of the methods used are carving, scratching, stamping, adding coils, slabs, or bits of clay.

Tools can be any that do the proper job, from a professional sgraffito tool to pencils, nails, or your hands. Even such basic means as pinching can be effective on certain forms. As you can see in the illustrations here, texture can enhance a shape, or it can dominate it.

Firing

After you have finished making a pot, the next step is to let it dry completely, so that all moisture is gone from the clay. The pot is then placed in a kiln or furnace which is heated to temperatures ranging from 650°C to 1300°C, depending on the type of clay body from which the pot was made. This is called firing, and the object here is to heat the elements in the clay until they fuse.

The colour of clay is also transformed during this process and what you had known in the workshop as a dull grey becomes a warm and appealing off-white buff, tan or dark red. Fired clay always has a matt surface; the glossy surface that you have seen on pottery is called glaze.

Rough textured vessel.

Interesting texture using slabs.

Stamp impressed decoration.

94

Clay

First among the secondary clays are the following: kaolins, ball clays, fireclays, stoneware clays, and earthenware clays. Most generally used by potters today are stoneware clays which generally fire to a light grey colour and mature between 1250°C and 1300°C. These result in ware that is hard and vitreous, ideal for pots that must be handled a great deal or withstand heat, such as cooking ware.

Kaolin. Sedimentary kaolin is a natural clay composed mainly of silica and alumina and when formed makes the finest whiteware body available.

Ball clay resembles kaolin, but is finer. When fired, it is almost white.

Fireclay resembles kaolin in chemical content, but contains more iron, causing the clay to turn buff-coloured when fired.

Stoneware is usually made from several natural clays plus alumina and silica. When fired, it becomes hard and vitreous, able to hold water without being glazed. It generally fires to a light grey.

Earthenware is usually made from a natural clay and is low fired, as opposed to stoneware which is high fired, maturing at a kiln temperature between 950°C and 1150°C. The body is non-vitreous and will not hold a liquid unless glazed. The colour after firing is usually buff or red.

Porcelain is made from a prepared body containing kaolin, ball clay, feldspar, and flint. Hard, white, translucent in thin areas, it requires the highest fire of all to 1450°C.

High fired porcelain bowl, unglazed.

Two contrasting earthenware vases.

Partially glazed stoneware teapot.

Firing process

Since the compounds which make up clay and glaze undergo many chemical changes during the firing cycle, this is a process that takes a certain amount of care. In this area, there is no substitute for actual experience. Depending upon the temperatures to which your kiln must be heated and *slowly* cooled, the firing cycle can take up to ten or even twelve hours. Firing to low earthenware temperatures should take eight hours, and never less than six.

Oxidation firing is the normal firing in all types of kilns. The kiln you use will be heated either by electricity, gas, or oil. An electric kiln *always* has an oxidizing fire since there is no combustible fuel to consume the oxygen, which is always present.

The results of oxidation are generally predictable, and you can obtain a wide range of bright and glossy colours with oxidation glazes. The common temperatures for oxidizing fire are under 1200°C.

Reduction firing is done during certain periods of the firing cycle in gas or oil kilns to develop the particular colour characteristics of reduction glazes. After beginning with oxidizing fire, the burners and air intake are so regulated as to get incomplete combustion, which releases carbon into the kiln. This is known as reducing the atmosphere. Since carbon has a great affinity for oxygen, it will, in this atmosphere, steal it from the iron and copper oxides which are part of reduction glazes. When either of these are deprived of their oxygen, they remain suspended in glaze as pure colloidal metal. The normally green copper glaze then becomes a luscious ruby red, occasionally flecked with blues and purples, while iron oxide loses its usual brownish-red colour and takes on a variety of quiet grey-green tones.

Reduction firing is best done at high temperatures – between 1200°C and 1300°C. Although the range of colours available with reduction glazes is small, they more than make up for this with their subtlety and quiet beauty.

Oxidation-fired stoneware vessel.

Rich glaze produced by reduction.

Glaze

Glaze produces a layer of glass crystals on the clay surface. Its purpose is both decorative and, since it waterproofs a vessel, useful. Glaze is applied in a liquid state, and when the pot is fired it reacts and melts forming a thin layer of glass. There are low-fire glazes, those which melt at 850°C to 1100°C, and high-fire glazes, those which need temperatures of 1150°C to 1300°C. Within these categories there are also many types: crackle, matt, crystalline, slip, lustre, reduction, and salt glazes.

The common procedure for glazing is first to bisque fire a pot – that is, fire it to a temperature of about 950°C. A raw, dry clay vessel is fragile, and a bisque firing makes it hard enough to be handled safely yet porous enough to absorb glaze readily. For a beginner prepared glazes are recommended, but remember that specific glazes are designed for certain clays and kiln temperatures.

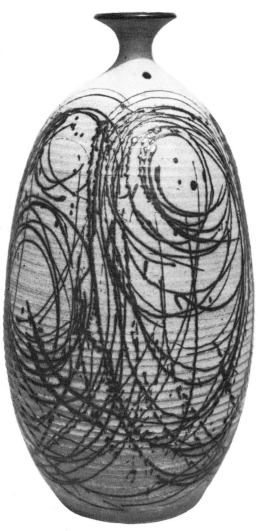

Slip trailing decoration on bottle.

Jar with varied glazed exterior.

Wax resist with matt glaze slip.

Materials and equipment

Only a few tools will be necessary. These are inexpensive and can be obtained from ceramics supply dealers or else improvised.

Ruler. Used for measuring or as a beater for shaping work.

Chinese brush. Ideal for applying glaze. Small paint brushes of various sizes can also be used.

Wire trimming tool. For shaping and carving pots.

Pin (mounted on a handle). Can be purchased, but a hat pin stuck through a cork will work as well.

Pencil. This has many uses.

Wire. For cutting through clay while wedging and slicing slabs. Attach a 610mm length to handles of some type – wood sticks, for instance.

'Fettling' or potter's knife. Best purchased, but a table knife or painter's palette knife will do.

Choosing clay. As to clay you will use, since different types fire at different temperatures, it is useful to know in advance what kind of kiln will be available to you. If you don't know the kind of kiln you will be using, the best solution is to choose a clay with a wide firing range, one that can be used successfully at different temperatures. Look for one which will fire from 1038°C to 1177°C. Although most professional potters make their own glazes, beginners should buy prepared ones. These are again determined by your clay and the firing range of the kiln you are using.

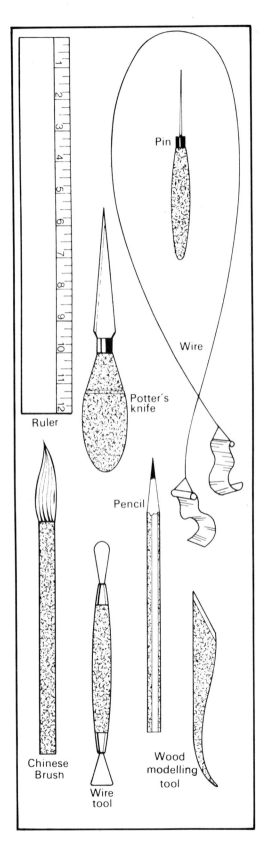

Ruler

Pin

Wire

Potter's knife

Pencil

Chinese Brush

Wire tool

Wood modelling tool

Wedging

Wedging gives you clay of a smooth even texture.

Take the lump of clay and cut it in half, either by pushing it against a wedging wire stretched across the tabletop or by holding a wire taut and pushing it through the clay.

Throw one half down hard on the table: then throw the other half on top of the first. 'Cut and slam' again and continue this procedure until all the air has been driven out of the clay. The clay is 'ready' when you can cut through it with a wire at any point and find it completely smooth. Store what you don't use immediately in a damp box or wrap in polythene. Once clay is wedged, it stays wedged, so there is no danger of doing work which will have to be repeated.

Making slabs

There are two ways of making slabs. In one, two guide sticks are placed, on a piece of hessian, as far apart as the slab is to be wide. The thickness of the sticks will determine the thickness of the slab, and I would suggest using sticks 15mm ($\frac{1}{2}$in) thick. Put a large ball of clay on the hessian between the sticks and roll it out with a rolling pin or dowel, resting whichever you use on the two pieces of wood. This will give you slabs of an even thickness.

Peel the clay off the hessian and trim the ragged edges.

Although hessian is used so that clay won't stick to the table, it also gives one side of the slab an interesting texture.

The other method of making slabs is to take a big hunk of prepared clay and, on a table or a flat surface, pound it into a rectangle the size of a shoe box. Slabs can then be sliced off the squared piece of clay with a wire. Although this approach will not give you completely even slabs, it is much faster.

Always give the slabs a chance to stiffen before using them.

Making coils

There are also two ways of making coils. For small, even ones roll out balls of clay on a freshly dampened table, so that the clay remains moist and does not break. Larger coils can be made by squeezing.

Clay ball for pinch method, rolling small coils and squeezing large coil into shape.

Slabs can be made by rolling out or by cutting them with a wire from a clay block.

they offer to the beginner the best way of acquiring a feeling for the clay. Take advantage of this 'getting acquainted' period before going to work on the slab and coil projects. The idea is basic: a ball of wedged clay is pressed or pinched into a small shape. For this version, texturing is added at the end to make a small-scale vase.

There are a number of ways you can use such pots, as containers for dried flowers or small fresh ones, as cigarette holders, or as holders for paper clips and pins.

If you are making a vase which will hold fresh flowers, you will at least have to glaze the inside of the pot. Follow the instructions on page 110. These will also tell you how to glaze the outside of the vase.

After glazing, the vase is ready to be fired. If you have made a number of pinch pots, you can at this point take them to your local kiln. Do not arrive with one pot in hand, no matter how proud you might be of your work, for firing a single piece is costly and impractical.

Pinch pot

The pinch method is about the simplest way to make a pot. Since these pots are usually small and do not require tools in the actual forming,

Form a ball by slapping and rolling clay. Rotate it in one hand and make opening with thumb of other hand, pinch walls to even thickness and desired shape. Work slowly and evenly for maximum control. Keep hands dry and avoid use of water.

For a narrow-topped vase, pleat walls at intervals and pinch them smoothly and symmetrically. A lip can be added by bending back top of walls and the pot may be decorated if so wished. Finally, tap bottom of pot gently on table to flatten.

Slab portfolio

Here are several examples of work done exclusively with slabs to show the versatility of this technique before you start slab projects of your own.

A tray can be made effectively by taking a slab and merely turning up the edges, or a simple plant pot by bending a slab into a cylindrical shape and boldly pinching the seam, as was done to make the pots in the photograph.

The hanging plant pot was made by pressing the centre of a slab into a shallow mould, then when the clay hardened, holes were cut for the cords from which it hangs.

Texture. Also remember surface effects can often be enhanced by overall texture – achieved by making the slab on hessian or some other coarse material or surface.

Cylindrical slab vase. This project gives you the opportunity to use a slab with an overall texture. Although a cylindrical vase such as this can be any height, the one here is about 178mm (7in) tall, perfect for many short-stemmed flowers. Because of the overall texture and the additional stamping and carving, the rich surface of this pot would look very well in unglazed clay, but the interior would have to be treated since the vase must hold water. In

the example shown, the stamping and carving were combined in one area, but you can make other designs.

Note: make the slab at least 13mm ($\frac{1}{2}$in) thick so that it will not crack when you bend it into a cylinder.

101

Covered jar

The purpose of this project is to give you the experience of making a four-sided piece with handles and cover.

An additional point of interest here is the pinching method of sealing the joins. Besides serving to cement the sides, this treatment is decorative.

After you have made the slabs necessary for the jar, let the clay dry until it is stiff but still wet enough so that you can pinch it. If you don't allow the slabs to stiffen, they may collapse during construction of the project. This applies to all slab work. Another general rule is to make all joins inside a slab pot as strong as possible by scoring and adding bits of fresh clay. That is, make scratches across the joining areas with your pin-on-stick tool or more practically, a fork. Then add bits of clay to the scored areas and push them into the scratches, smoothing over the seam with your fingers. Since the finishing of a slab pot usually cannot be done until the clay is very stiff (but not leather-hard), it is advisable to work on more than one piece at a time.

With a wire cut six slabs from block of clay (see page 99) each about 127mm × 254mm and 13mm thick. Score edges with pin tool or fork and moisten them with soft clay.

Add slip to the edges of two slabs and join edges as shown; work them together with a modelling tool. Continue assembling slabs in this manner. If necessary, a coil of clay can be applied to each seam and worked in to reinforce the join.

The fourth slab must be stiff enough to support itself during application. Turn four sides onto another slab for base and cut off excess clay. Join the sides and base on the inside. Pinch outer seams for extra strength and as decoration.

Cut a piece of clay about 50mm × 205mm and wrap it round the top of the jar. Work in with fettling knife from the inside. Cut two strips for handles and attach, top ends first, to sides using knife and fingers. Cut two similar strips for lid.

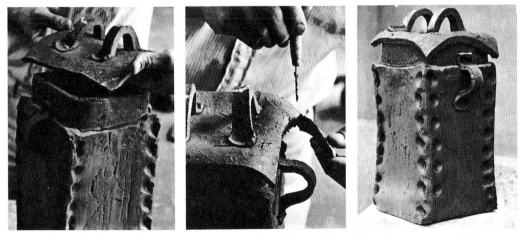

For the lid, cut slab about 152mm square. It will mould itself to the contours of the neck. Trim cover to correct proportions when in position. Allow jar to dry thoroughly, and glaze and fire it (remove lid during drying and firing).

Coil portfolio

The building of coil upon coil was the way primitive man made his pots, and it was this easy method of gradual building that eventually suggested the wheel.

At one period, coil work was done in a turntable on the ground, rotating it and laying on a rope of coil which another craftsman would make and feed to him over his shoulder. The man at the turntable soon learned that if water and pressure were used when the turntable was rotated, the walls of a pot would rise and become thinner. Potters later discovered from using the turntable that clay could be made to rise without the use of coils. With speed, water, and the proper handling, clay could be thrown and pulled up. Thus, the potter's wheel evolved, and production became much faster. Because of the feeling of structure which you can get with coils, the next few projects will give you work different in feeling from the slab exercises. The coil itself can be allowed to show or it can be smoothed over.

CREAM JUG

Small coils will be used for this project since they are easier for the beginner to manipulate. The pitcher will only be 152 or 178mm (6 or 7in) high and will be rolled rather than pinched into shape.

For one jug you will need up to twelve coils, each approximately

Pat out a small slab of clay about the size of the palm of your hand. Cut a circle from it and remove excess clay. Build up the walls of the pot with clay coils, joining the coils on the inside of the pot with a modelling tool. Direct coils outward at top to form a spout. Braid three thin coils to make a handle.

When the handle is completed, flatten it with a small stick or a ruler. Attach the handle directly behind the spout, joining the top end first, and then smoothing the clay to the coiled body of the pitcher. The pot is now ready to be dried, glazed and fired. Remember that it must be glazed inside to be water retaining.

305mm (12in) long, but make twice this number and work on two jugs simultaneously.

During coiling, one jug may begin to weaken, and you will have to stop and let it stiffen for a while before beginning again.

To make coils roll out balls of clay on a slightly damp board, working with both hands from the centre outwards. A damp board is particularly necessary when making small coils since it prevents them from drying out and breaking.

Cover the finished coils with a damp cloth. The jug will also have to be glazed on the inside, whether you are going to use it at the table or as a small vase. The outside need not.

PATIO BOTTLE

Coils can be used on a wheel-built pot to increase its size – a pot is thrown to its maximum height, large coils are joined on and built up to make the pot larger – but exclusive use of coils is the best way of making the bottle in this project, shown overleaf. It is about 1m (3ft) tall. Make sure that you have a large enough kiln available to fire it. If you don't have a kiln large enough, adapt the project to the size that is available to you. If you like, you can take several days to finish the bottle, covering the top with a sheet of plastic each time you stop. The base will then be able to dry out while the upper part remains damp and workable.

For base, roll out lump of clay into circular shape about 305mm in diameter and cut into an even circle. Form large snake-like ropes of clay about 25mm thick by squeezing with the hands. Build walls by winding clay ropes round circular base. Pinch each coil securely to the previous one. If work has to be interrupted, be sure to deeply score the top of the pot before beginning again.

Score all the coils on the inside to make a good join all around. When the desired height is reached cut a slab strip large enough for two handles about 64mm wide, 203mm long and 13mm thick, and shape to the bottle. Add a rim of 25mm thick clay and smooth by patting with a stick. Such a large piece must be given longer to dry before being glazed and fired.

Coil-built patio bottle, an excitingly large project for a beginner to do.

Stamp-decorated candle holder involving both coil and slab techniques.

106

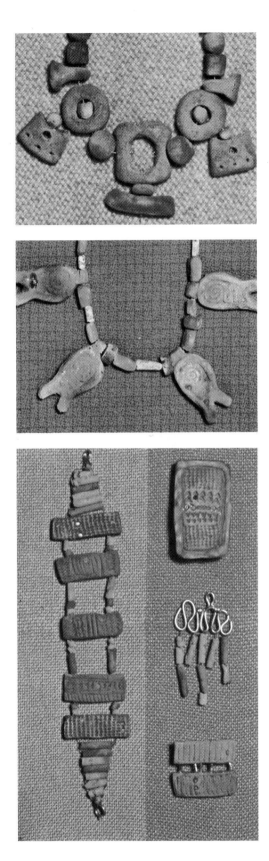

Left: detail of unglazed necklace.

Middle left: pre-coloured Egyptian paste with incised designs.

Bottom left: Bracelet, pins, earrings.

Below: Necklace of pre-coloured Egyptian paste and grapefruit seeds.

Candleholder

Two basic techniques and a decorative device – slab, coil, and the plaster stamp – are combined to make an arc-shaped candleholder. This is another project which lends itself to many variations, and feel free to make your own adaptations. As you begin to master many of the basic principles of pottery you no doubt will have more confidence in your abilities to work out original designs.

A series of candleholders following the basic plan could be made, with different placement of the coil holders. And the base slab does not have to curve in. It could remain a rectangle or take the form of a gentle S-shape. Since this is not a time-consuming project, play around with it before deciding on a piece, or pieces, to be glazed and fired. Don't labour too hard on any one; the more spontaneous the approach, the better the result.

Prepare slab of wedged clay 254mm × 127mm and small coils. Stamp, cut out and lift.

Circle a coil into a cylinder just wider than a candle (fired clay contracts). Attach cylinder to slab by scoring cylinder's base. Smooth join or leave marks for decoration. Prepare short coils for sides. Cut at an angle to fit the slope of slab, and attach.

Make another coil cylinder for the top and attach it as you did the previous one. When the piece is dry it is ready to be glazed and fired. A finished example is shown on page 106, but this can be varied according to taste and available stamps.

Egyptian paste jewellery

This interesting and intriguing process was handed down from ancient times. It is necessary here to use Egyptian paste that is commercially purchased or that is made from the recipe given.

Material. The name Egyptian paste comes from a combination of clay and glaze that the ancients used for their distinctive ceramic beads. Modern potters have not been able to duplicate the Egyptian recipe, but we have come up with something quite similar. Although it feels like and can be worked the same as ordinary clay - rolled in balls, pinched into squares, patted into slabs and cut - it eliminates half the steps since glaze is already part of the clay body.

There are two recipes for Egyptian paste. One fires with a dry matt finish, and the beads can be fired together in a bowl without sticking. Both recipes, however, only require one firing to arrive at the finished result. The second recipe gives a jewellery that has a glossy, glaze-like finish. Beads made with this recipe must be strung on nichrome wire rather than placed inside pots when fired.

Below are recipes for both versions, as well as the various colourants which can be added. The ingredients can be purchased from the ceramic suppliers. You need only mix them with water until you have a clay-like substance.

Roll paste into coils.

Cut into pieces, shape and bore holes.

Paste beads ready for firing.

EGYPTIAN PASTE RECIPES ORTON CONE 06–04

Dry – Beads will not stick together when fired

MATT BASE

Silica	75 grams
Copper carbonate	2
Sodium bicarbonate	2
Bentonite	8
Frit, lead	20

Shiny – Beads must be strung on nichrome wire when fired:

GLOSS BASE

Oxford spar	800 grams
Flint	400
China clay	500
Ball clay	100
Sodium bicarbonate	120
Soda ash	120
Whiting	100
Fine white sand	160

COLOURANTS – FOR BOTH RECIPES

Green	3% Chrome
Turquoise	3% Black copper oxide
Blue	1%–3% Cobalt carbonate
Black	3% Manganese dioxide
Brown	3% Red iron oxide

Dipped

Sprayed

Glazing pots

Following are the four most common methods of applying glaze. Keep in mind that the bottom of a piece is left unglazed, so that it will not stick to the kiln shelf during firing. Either clean off bottom or paint with melted wax before glazing the piece.

Dipping is probably the simplest method, but it requires a large amount of glaze.

To glaze a pot one colour, hold it at an angle and dip it into the glaze, turning it quickly and holding it so that as much of the pot as possible is covered. Do not let the layer of glaze become too thick. Touch up unglazed areas with a brush.

When glaze is desired only on the outside of a pot, hold the pot by the base and dip straight up and down. The air trapped inside will prevent the glaze from entering.

Pouring is done when a pot is too large to dip or the amount of glaze available is too little.

To coat the inside of a pot, pour glaze in until the pot is one-third filled. Twirl the pot around and pour out the excess. Do this quickly since the correct thickness of freshly applied glaze is that of a playing card.

For the outside, lay the pot on two sticks placed over a basin. Pour glaze evenly over and around the pot.

Brushed

Brushed

Spraying gives an even coating to the pot and more control over thickness but it often wastes large amounts of glaze. It is recommended chiefly for large pots with deep surface depressions and for applying transparent or coloured glazes.

At times it is hard to tell how thick the glaze is, and the best way to check is by scratching it with a pin.

Note: as many glaze materials are toxic, spraying should be done in a booth with a fan or out of doors.

Brushing is generally used for decorative panels, bands of glaze, etc, but can also be employed for covering an entire pot. Use a wide brush with soft bristles and flow on several coats of glaze for an even application. Apply each coat in a different direction. It is advisable to glaze the inside of a pot first. You can then turn it upside down and work on the outside without disturbing the interior.

Oxides or other colourants for decorative designs are best applied with a brush, over the initial glaze. It helps to have a turntable so that a pot can be rotated while glaze, oxides, and other colourants are applied.

Decorating techniques

The method of surface texture described earlier was for clay still in the plastic state. There are, in addition, ways of decorating clay when it is leather-hard, dry, or even after it has been bisque fired.

Wax-resist decoration can be effectively used when clay is in the dry state or after it has been bisque fired. A design is painted on the clay with a solution of thinned wax. When glaze is applied, it will run off the wax areas, giving a design in the

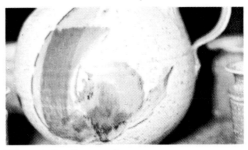
Wax-resist decoration

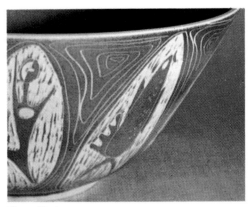
Sgraffito

Stained

Slip trailed

111

Dipping base of pot into glaze.

Pouring glaze onto squat jar.

Applying glaze with a spray.

Bands and circles added by brushing.

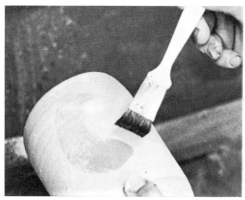

A stage in wax-resist decoration.

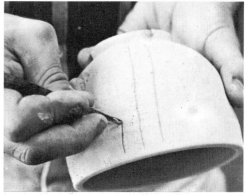

Lines incised for sgraffito work.

Staining part of a ceramic plaque.

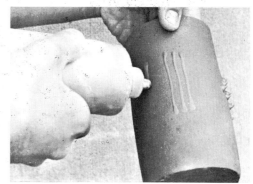

Trailing lines of slip on pot.

clay body colour surrounded by glaze.

The wax need not only be applied to the dry or bisqued clay, but also may be brushed on a layer of glaze with a second coat of glaze sprayed on top. Any wax can be heated in a double boiler over a hot plate and used. Commercial water-soluble wax emulsions are more convenient but give no better results than any paraffin wax.

Sgraffito is a technique also used on both hard and bisque-fired clay. If wax has been applied, a design scratched through the wax with a sgraffito tool gives a sharp linear pattern. More common is to scratch a design through the glaze coating of a pot to expose either the body or a preliminary glaze. This is done while the glaze is still slightly damp. If too dry or too thick, it will chip and leave a ragged edge. The object of sgraffito is a sharp, clean line.

Staining is best done when the clay is dry. This is a way of treating clay when you want a burnt, natural looking surface.

To make a stain, use two tablespoons of any oxide (such as red iron oxide), the same amount of high or low fire glaze, and half a cup of water.

Mix and paint on the area you want stained. Wipe off with a damp sponge. Any impression in the clay will be darker and the raised surfaces lighter after firing.

Slip trailing is a technique in which slip is trailed over leather-hard clay with a syringe, in much the same way as decorating a cake. The body must not be too dry, however, or the slip will fall off when it dries. A plastic mustard dispenser (shown here) can be as effective as a syringe, and colourants may be added to the slip if desired.

Firing a kiln

When loading the kiln be sure the glazed pieces are not touching.

Always give the kiln a preliminary heating with the door open to allow the physically combined water to escape from the clay. Heating time should be at least two hours for raw ware, and more for large or especially heavy pieces.

Let the temperature in the kiln rise gradually and uniformly, for if the pots are heated too quickly, they will explode; let the cooling-off time be at least double the firing time. Never open the door of a kiln until the temperature is down to at least 200°C and never open it completely or attempt to unload a kiln until it has dropped to at least 150°C.

Firing to low earthenware temperatures should take eight hours; stoneware needs up to ten.

Before purchasing a small electric kiln, check its voltage to be sure your house wiring circuits are adequate to handle it. Take the same safety precautions in firing a kiln as you would when using any other high voltage appliance.

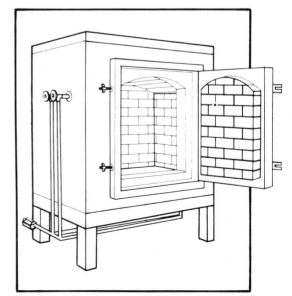

A typical brick-lined kiln.

DRIED FLOWERS

There is no cause for sadness at the end of summer for practically every kind of plant material in the garden or countryside, can be dried in some form.

Conditions have to be just right for harvest. Ideally, all plant material for drying should be gathered on a dry day, after the morning dew has evaporated in the sun. But since you will be harvesting from the early spring – for the seed capsules of the small species bulbs – to the late autumn and even beyond, and since this is not an ideal world, you will have to gather material as and when you can. It is better to capture a basketful of seedheads which are not quite ready than to watch the next storm batter them to the ground.

If you have to collect rain-soaked plant material, shake it gently and lay it on sheets of blotting paper or newspaper, turning it over until all the excess moisture has been absorbed by the paper.

Hang drying

Any dry, dark, airy room is suitable for this method. Slow drying causes fading; therefore warmth and dark are essential for the best results.

Remove the leaves first. They do not dry well by this method, and only serve to increase the moisture content of the room as they do so. The leaves need not be discarded, though; they can be dried by pressing.

Tie flowers and seedheads in bunches

according to type. The stems will shrink as the material dries and the cord or twine will need to be tightened to prevent flowers and seedheads from falling to the floor. Use gardeners' twine or raffia – not coarse string – and tie a slip knot which can be pulled tighter without being untied and retied. Very fine and delicate stems should be tied with silk thread, split raffia or gardeners' ties.

SUITABLE MATERIAL

Acanthus or Bear's Breeches (Acanthus species). Hardy perennial. Dry the tall sweeping arcs of pink, white and mauve flower heads in a warm room. Good for designs where height is needed.

Achillea or Yarrow (Achillea species). Hardy perennial. Flowers can be dried upside down or upright in containers. Pick when flower heads are young.

Acroclinium (Helipterum). Half-hardy annual. An everlasting flower in yellow, white and pink. Grows to a height of about 30 centimetres (one foot).

Allium. From the small, round clover-like flowers of the chive to A. Moly (garlic), which produces bright yellow umbrella-shaped flowers, these bulbous herbs are invaluable for flower design. Hang-dry chive flowers; dry the flowers of the garlic upright or flat. Onion heads,

too, large balls of blue-mauve flowers, can be hang-dried.

Bells of Ireland (Molucella laevis). Half-hardy annual. Remove the leaves and dry the 18-inch spikes of olive green bells. They gradually become as stiff as paper cones and fade to a rich creamy parchment colour. Can also be preserved in glycerine.

Bluebell (Scilla). Pick the heads when they are already becoming dry and papery and hang until the process is complete. Can also be dried upright in a container.

Bulrush. Grows in and around ponds and on marshy land. Pick the long, poker-straight spikes when they are half developed.

Burdock. The burrs of this plant, often a bristly and prickly irritant on a country walk, dry well and keep their colour.

Carrot. One of the few leaves dried successfully hanging upside down.

Chinese Lanterns or Cape Gooseberry (Physalis franchetii). Hardy perennial. Dry the seedheads. Cut when the calyces have not all ripened. Use in sprays or snip off individual seedheads and use for dried-flower pictures or designs on pre-formed shapes (flower balls, cones, door wreaths and so on).

Clarkia. Hardy annual. The white, pink and purple flowers dry extremely well and keep their colour. Can also be dried flat.

Clematis (C. Vitalba is known as Old Man's Beard or Traveller's Joy). Hardy perennial. These flowers give a good range of deep colour – strong mauve, purple and pink. If you do

not cut the flowers in time to dry them, you have a second chance because many varieties have large, fluffy seedheads which dry well, too.

Columbine (Aquilegia). Hardy perennial. Harvest the seedheads as soon as they open and start curving outwards, but not before.

Delphinium and Larkspur. Hardy perennial and annual. Dry both flowers and seedheads – a difficult choice to make. Pick flowers for drying when some buds are still unopened and dry in a heated room. Seedheads can also be dried flat.

Dock. Can be found in ditches and on waste land. The whorl-shaped seedheads change from lime green to deep red when dried. Can also be preserved in glycerine.

Foxglove (Digitalis). Hardy annual, biennial and perennial. Can be found growing wild, or cultivated. Dry the seedheads which often grow in gently curving S shape.

Glixia. These everlasting flowers, with minute star-like heads, can be bought dyed in bright colours. The honey, ginger brown and pale cream colours seem to complement other dried materials best.

Globe Artichoke (Cynara scolymus). The huge purple flower heads, like great thistles, dry well and turn glistening cream.

Globe Thistle (Echinops ritro). Hardy perennial. Cut the steel-blue globular flower heads as they are just beginning to open. Leave them any longer and they will disintegrate as they dry.

Golden Rod (Solidago). Hardy perennial. Dry the long flower spikes either hanging upside down or up-right in a container. Cut stems in a range of sizes to give flexibility to arrangements.

Grasses. Some grasses can be dried by hanging upside down but most give more satisfactory results when flat-dried on trays or box lids. If there is any doubt about the stems being strong enough to hold the weight of the heads, then it is better to dry the material horizontally.

Heaths and Heathers (Erica and Calluna). Hardy shrubs. Pick the stems when the flowers have just opened. May be dried by hanging or standing upright in water. Some flowers turn an attractive brown, others stay white.

Helichrysum or Straw Daisies. Half-hardy annual or half-hardy shrub. These everlasting flowers, in a wide range of colours from pale cream to deep burgundy, are among the most useful of dried plant material. Some arrangers recommend binding each stem with wire before drying.

Hollyhock (Althaea). Hardy perennial. If you do not cut the flowers in time to preserve them, then you can dry the long stems of seed heads by hanging or laying flat.

Honesty (Lunaria). Hardy biennial. The dried silvery-moon seedpods have an ethereal, translucent quality. Cut the stems when the centre layer, like silver tissue-paper, is still protected by two brown outer skins. When you are ready to arrange the sprays, rub these layers off between thumb and first finger.

Hop (Humulus). Hardy annual. H. Lupulus is the common hop, often found twining round fences and poles and in hedges. It can be dried by hanging upside down or preserving in glycerine. The pale olive green flowers fade only slightly and the individual papery blossoms are useful in picture designs.

Lavender (Lavandula). Hardy shrub. For drying, cut the stems before the flowers are fully open and hang upside down or leave in a little water without replenishing.

Love-in-a-mist (Nigella). Hardy annual. Pretty as the pink, white or blue flowers are, one is reluctant to cut them and sacrifice the dramatic seedheads which are almost globular and vary from cream *to reddish purple. Some are striped in those colours. Remove most of the frondy fennel-type leaves, but leave a few near the seedhead to frame it.

Lupin (Lupinus). Hardy perennial. Cut stems of varying length, some straight and some curved.

Maize or Sweet corn. When the cob has ripened and been cut, the long spikes of seedheads and the husk which enclosed the cob can be hung-dried. The husks take on the appearance of crêpe paper and dry to a pale avocado green colour.

Mallow (Lavatera). Hardy annual. Pink or white flowers are replaced by pale silver-grey seedheads like closed-up stars.

Nipplewort (Lapsana). A weed in the garden, it is not found in a seedman's catalogue, but is highly valuable in arrangements. Gather as soon as the flowers are over and the seedheads beginning to open. Dry upside down or flat.

Onion (Allium). Dry the large round seedheads.

Pampas Grass (Cortaderia). Hardy perennial. The huge, soft, feathery spikes, surely the most majestic of all grasses, should be cut before they start to shed. If this is not possible, they can be kept in shape by spraying with ordinary hair lacquer.

Poppy (Papaver). Hardy annual. All kinds of poppy, from the tiny ones found growing wild to the much larger cultivated varieties, provide excellent seedheads which are invaluable dried material.

Rhodanthe. Half-hardy annual. These pinky-white cone-shaped everlasting flowers retain their colour well when dried.

Russian Vine. Cut the flowers as soon as they open and hang in a dark room.

Sea Holly (Eryngium). Hardy perennial. Dry the pale blue, round flower heads on the stems, with the leaves.

Sea Lavender or Statice (Limonium). Hardy perennial. The small sprays of faded-lavender blue, pink or green everlasting flowers dry well.

Senecio. Hardy annual and half-hardy shrub. The annual has loose clusters of red, pink, lilac or white flowers and the shrub, a creeper, yellow heads which flower in December. The flowers dry to a warm yellowy brown, the leaves silver on one side and sage green on the other.

Smoke tree (Rhus). Dry the seedheads of this tree which live up to the name and, when dried, look like a puff of smoke.

Stonecrop (Sedum). Hardy perennial. Flowers dry to a subtle pinky-beige in soft sprays.

Sycamore. Any tree which produces seeds in the form of 'keys' is worth watching. They should be cut before they are ripe and start floating down to the ground.

Teasel (Dipsacus). Hardy biennial. These long stems with seedheads like hairbrushes are often found on waste land. They dry well.

Thistle (Onopordon). Hardy perennial. Scotch or Cotton thistles, with their intriguing and intricate formation, are exciting materials to use in dried plant designs.

Xeranthemum. Hardy annual. Everlasting flowers with strong, wiry stems. Retain colour well after drying.

Drying in desiccants

Many flowers can be preserved in a desiccant. That is to say the flower is completely immersed in a material which gradually draws the moisture from it.

There are several different types of desiccant and the one you use might well depend on local availability.

Borax. The lightest in weight, and therefore the most suitable for delicate flowers, is household borax, available in 450g (1lb) packs from chemists and hardware stores. This should not be confused with the medical quality of borax, which costs more. The principle when using borax, as with all other desiccants, is to cover the flower completely, shaking and working the material under, between and on top of all the petals so that there is not even a minute air pocket preventing the desiccant from coming into contact with the surface of the flower. Be-

cause of its lightness, borax is a little difficult to work into the flower and can be gently pushed into the cavities with a small camelhair paintbrush. It can be used with an equal quantity of cornmeal.

Sand is a readily absorbent material and has been used successfully to dry flowers for generations. However it needs thorough washing before it is ready to use. To do this, put the sand into a bucket, fill with water, stir well, and pour off the excess. Fill the bucket again, add a little household detergent, stir to distribute the cleaner, then pour off the water. Rinse the sand several times in fresh water, until finally the water poured away is clear. Spread out the sand on trays and dry in the sun or in the oven at a very low temperature. This will take 3–4 hours.

Sand is considerably heavier than household borax and will run freely and smoothly between the flower petals. Care should be taken to support the flower from underneath while this is being done, or the weight of the sand could be damaging.

Silica gel crystals are rather large and they should be ground before being used to dry flowers; you can easily crush them with a rolling pin. Since this material can absorb up to fifty per cent of its own weight in moisture, the granules must be dried before they are ready to use again. To do this, spread them in a baking tray in a low oven until the litmus paper indicator, sold with the substance, turns blue.

Method

Whichever desiccant is used, the method is the same.

Pour a layer of desiccant over the bottom of an airtight container, such as a lidded polythene sandwich box, a cake tin or a large used coffee tin.

Push the short stem of a flower into the material and, supporting the flower underneath with the fingers of one hand, gently and slowly pour on the desiccant, working it well in between the petals. The success of the drying operation will depend on the care taken at this stage. If some of the petals are not completely covered, damp spots and eventually mildew will result.

Add a second and third flower to the container, covering it in the same way, but making sure that it does not touch any other flower.

Pour on a further 4–5cm ($1\frac{1}{2}$–2in) of the desiccant and cover the box securely. If you are in any doubt about its airtight properties, stick a strip of self-adhesive tape round the rim of the lid.

Move the container, very carefully, without tipping, to a place where it will not be disturbed and leave it for at least one day, or according to the type of flower being dried.

Timing

The following table is a general reference guide to approximate drying times. The exact time will depend to a great extent on the size and moisture content of each flower and the temperature of the room. A dry warm room gives the best results. To test for readiness, slowly pour off the desiccant if there is only one flower in the box. If there are more, gently work your fingers under the desiccant and lift out one of the flowers, supporting it from below. Shake the material from the petals. They should make a slight rustling sound when touched. If they do not, return the flower carefully, covering it completely again with the desiccant. Test again the next day.

When the flowers are ready to be removed, gently shake off the excess material by holding each one upside down. If any desiccant remains on the petals – borax is the more likely to adhere to the flower – brush it off carefully with a fine paint-brush.

SUITABLE MATERIAL

Broom (Cytisus or Genista). Hardy shrub. Cut when not quite in full bloom. Lay short sprays flat. Retains both colour and shape well.

Carnation (Dianthus caryophyllus). Hardy perennial. Cut before fully in bloom.

Daisy (Bellis). Hardy perennial. Stems need wiring before drying.

Forsythia. Hardy shrub. Dry short sprays horizontally.

Hyacinth. Stems need wiring.

Laburnum. Hardy tree. See Broom.

Larkspur and Delphinium. Hardy perennial. Dry small young shoots.

Lilac (Syringa). Hardy perennial. Dries very well.

Lily of the Valley (Convallaria). Hardy perennial. 'Fades' to a deep cream.

London Pride (Saxifraga umbrosa). Hardy perennial. Very useful shape.

Marigold (Calendula and Tagetes). Half-hardy annual. Stems need wiring. Dry face down.

Pink (Dianthus). Hardy perennial. Retains colour very well.

Pansy (Viola wittrockiana). Hardy perennial. Stems need wiring.

Polyanthus (Primula). Hardy perennial. Push wire into calyx to prevent flower heads falling off.

Rose. Small buds give best results.

Stock. Double flowers are prettiest.

Sweet pea (Lathyrus). Hardy annual. Red colours strengthen considerably.

Violet (Viola). Hardy annual. Keeps colour well.

Wallflower. Hardy biennial. Sprays may be lain flat.

Zinnia. Half-hardy annual. Dry face down. Small varieties dry best.

Push flower stems into desiccant.

Gently pour on more desiccant.

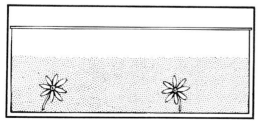

Cover box with an airtight lid.

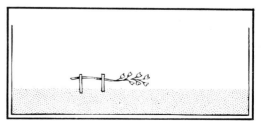

Store delicate sprays as shown.

A country kitchen display given height by exotic pampas grass.

Dried seedheads can rival flowers in prettiness.

Pressing flowers and leaves

The process of pressing plants is a simple one. It is a matter of collecting plant material on a dry day, laying it carefully between two sheets of blotting paper, weighting it down and leaving in a warm, dry place for at least four to six weeks.

It is important to press all the material, but most particularly delicate flowers that would quickly wilt, absolutely fresh.

If you do want to press flowers which have thick centres, pull off each individual petal, press them singly so that no two are touching on the page, and reassemble them again for a life-like effect. Trumpet-shaped flowers, such as bluebells, can be sliced in half and then pressed.

You can buy simple flower presses, often in toy shops since the hobby is so popular with children.

The time-honoured method, however, is still perfectly satisfactory: sheets of blotting paper interleaved between the pages of a large book.

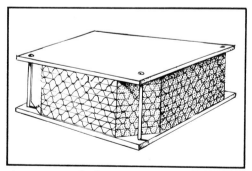

A press can be bought or made.

Press only one kind of plant material on each layer or page. Arrange it carefully so that no single leaf or flower touches another one.

Use a pair of fine tweezers to move the material, pushing one blade well under the flower or leaf so that you grasp it firmly in the centre. Dragging it along by the edge is likely to cause damage. Carefully cover the sheet of blotting paper with another, bringing it down slowly so that you do not create a rush of air. Label each section clearly before covering it with another layer of the press or folding the book.

The drying process continues for up to a year and the longer material is left the thinner it will become. Longer pressing has one great benefit: it makes the stronger-coloured flowers and petals more resistant to fading when they are brought out into the light.

SUITABLE MATERIALS
Berberis. Press the leaves singly.

Blackberry (Rubus). Press leaves singly or in sprays of three.

Broom (Cytisus). Press sprays.

Buttercup (Ranunculus). To press stalks, bend them between thumb and first finger to give 'movement' to the shape. Press flowers separately.

Camomile (Anthemis). Flowers fade to a soft cream when pressed; press stalks separately.

Campanula. Snip out centres.

Clematis. All varieties, including the wild ones, are suitable. Press flowers, leaves, stalks separately.

Cow Parsley. Press down well in the centre to flatten. When dried, they are like exquisite snowflakes. Treat these flowers with care.

Daffodil. One fresh flower equals two pressed ones. Separate the petals, cut the trumpet in half before treating. Reassemble in pictures.

Daisy (Bellis). Very thick-centred flowers are not suitable. All others respond well.

Dogwood (Cornus). The leaves are variegated green and cream.

Ferns. All kinds are good subjects for pressing. Very large leaves can be snipped into smaller sprays.

Globe thistle (Echinops). The dramatic outline of the leaves is invaluable in a collection.

Grasses. All types of grass, except thick, stubby heads, press well, and are very versatile in pressed flower pictures and other designs.

Hellebore (Helleborus corsicus). The long, thin leaves have pronounced veins when dried.

Honeysuckle (Lonicera). Press leaves and flowers separately.

Hydrangea. The florets fade to soft colours, green, pink or blue.

Ivy (Hedera). Press leaves of all sizes, from the smallest you can find.

Lamb's ear (Stachys). Press the white woolly leaves.

Maidenhair fern (Adiantum). Light as a feather, these leaves can only be handled on very still days.

Michaelmas daisy (Aster). Press flowers. Need heavy weight to flatten centre.

Marigold (Calendula). Snip out some centres before pressing – they are useful by themselves – and press some petals individually.

Narcissus. Dismantle flowers, press parts separately then reassemble.

Oak (Quercus). Press leaves.

Pansy (Viola). Press petals separately. The deep blue flowers will unfortunately fade to cream after exposure to strong light.

Pelargonium. Press leaves.

Primrose (Primula). Press stalks and flowers separately.

Raspberry (Rubus). Pick some leaves which are red-and-green coloured, and silver-backed, in a range of sizes.

Rock geranium. Press leaves.

Rose. Press petals separately. White ones will 'fade' to cream; red ones turn brown.

Rowan or mountain ash (Sorbus). Press the leaves only.

Santolina or Lavender Cotton. Small sprigs dry well.

Senecio (Ligularia). A useful two-toned material in silver and green.

Smoke tree or Sumach (Rhus). Pick at intervals to collect the leaves in a range of colours.

Thyme, wild. Strip off lower leaves and press short sprays.

Tulip (Tulipa). Press petals singly.

Violet (Viola). Press the flowers.

Virginia creeper (Vitis). Pick leaves of all sizes. They give warm, glowing red tones.

Yarrow (Achillea Millefolium). Very good for large picture designs. Press the umbrella-shaped heads and the leaves separately.

Cow parsley

Fern

Clover

Honeysuckle

Daisy

Wild thyme

Clematis montana

'Painting' with flowers

If you have already made some greeting cards and other small mementoes for friends, and have got the feel of working with pressed flowers, it is time to design a picture – probably the aim of everyone who has built up a sizeable collection of pressed material.

It does not really matter whether you fit your pressed flower picture to an existing frame or have one made to fit round it; there is a slight advantage to having the frame made first, because then you will have the glass exactly the size of your picture background, and can place it over blotting paper on top of your work each time you have to be interrupted. The best material to use as a background is artist's mounting board, which you can buy in a range of colours.

For all but the lightest pieces of natural material, for which you can use rubber solution, you should use a transparent adhesive.

As always, experiment with your design *before* sticking it down. Mark out the size of the background on a spare piece of card or fabric and move your materials around until you achieve a pleasing balance. If the design is a complicated one, make a rough sketch of it and mark and number the position of each leaf and flower.

Study each type of leaf and flower you intend to use and see what, in design terms, it is capable of. Try sticking some damaged examples on to a spare piece of card to check whether a leaf can be stuck at each end without cracking in the middle; if a flower can be laid on its side without folding over in half, and so on. See where the material touches the card, or how one piece fits on top of another, and note the touch points. These, and only these, are the spots where you will apply the adhesive.

Always allow one piece to dry before placing another on top of it. If a leaf seems inclined to curl up and away from the background, weight it with a coin or two until it is set in place. If you want to set a flower half on its side, at an angle of about 45 degrees, and it looks as if it will topple over as soon as you take your fingers away, prop it up with a few coins or a piece of twig until the adhesive strengthens enough to hold it. Then gently remove the props and admire the flower which looks as if it is being gently swayed downwards by the wind.

Apply adhesive very sparingly on the touch spots. To get the merest trace of the glue, 'wind' some from a tube or tin round the end of a spent matchstick or cocktail stick and apply it from there. Spread the end of the stick in a quick, narrow line along a stalk, making sure that it only touches the under surface and does not extend up and over the sides. Put only the tiniest dab on the ends of petals, just a touch on the part of a flower which lies flat.

*Delightful little sachets and cushions
(above and left) which can be filled with dry pot-pourri,
lavender or rose petals.*

Pot-pourri

Making pot-pourri is a wonderfully romantic way of storing up memories of the fragrance, colour and beauty of a garden. Lifting the lid from a bowl of dried petals and leaves is like taking the stopper off a bottle of expensive scent; yet infinitely more personal, because you can make pot-pourri from your own favourite flowers and scented leaves, spices and oils.

There are two kinds of pot-pourri, made by what are known as the dry and the moist methods. The dry method could not be simpler. It is just dried petals and leaves, a sprinkling of spice – any spice – and a little fixative stirred together and left to mature.

Moist pot-pourri

The principle of making moist pot-pourri is to mix dried petals, flowers and leaves with common salt, add a fixative such as powdered orris root or gum benzedrine (both still available), spices and flower oils. The traditional pure extracts of musk, bergamot, lavender, jasmine, rosemary, thyme, violet and attar of roses are not easy to come by now; when you can find them in old-fashioned shops with an aura of nostalgia, they are expensive. However, oil-based perfume essences give excellent results. You can also try culinary essences such as lemon, vanilla and almond; even lemon juice and brandy. With the addition, in the moist method, of these oils and essences, it is not as important to choose petals and leaves for their fragrance, as this will be enhanced and enriched by the oils. You can, therefore, include in your mixture a high proportion of flowers, like larkspur florets and marigolds, pansies and nasturtium, chosen simply for their colour or shape. Pot-pourri can be an on-going art and is by no means confined to summer flowers. You can dry the sweet-smelling spring flowers and store them in sealed polythene bags or lidded boxes ready to be blended with the summer blossoms as they come. As you add more flowers to your pot-pourri from time to time, add a little more orris root powder and spice, a few drops of flower oil or essence and bring your pot-pourri to life all over again.

Ingredients

200g (8oz) flowers, leaves and herbs, mixed.
100g (4oz) common household salt.
50g (2oz) powdered orris root.
$12\frac{1}{2}$g ($\frac{1}{2}$oz) ground cinnamon.
$12\frac{1}{2}$g ($\frac{1}{2}$oz) ground allspice.
$12\frac{1}{2}$g ($\frac{1}{2}$oz) ground cloves.
$\frac{1}{2}$ teaspoon grated nutmeg.
thinly pared rind of 1 lemon and 1 small orange.
1 vanilla pod.
Flower oil or essence.
1 teaspoon brandy (optional).

Gathering

On a dry day, gather a total of 200g (8oz) of flower petals and heads, scented leaves and herbs. For their scent, choose fragrant red rose petals, picking them at their best before they are ready to fall, and a selection from summer jasmine, buddleia, carnation, rosemary flowers and lavender, and spring flowers such as wallflower, narcissus and hyacinth.

For colour and shape, choose violets (which quickly lose their scent), pansies, marigolds and florets of larkspur and delphinium. Adapt this list to a well-balanced mixture of fragrance and colour from the flowers available, according to the season and what you have in your garden.

For the scented leaves, choose from bay, thyme, sage, marjoram, verbena, balm, bergamot, mint, rosemary, rose-scented and lemon-scented geranium leaves.

Method
Strip the petals from large flowers and leave the small ones whole. Spread them on small box lids, each flower type separate, and leave in hot sun to dry. Bring indoors overnight and put in the sun again the next day. The flowers will dry at different rates, according to their size and moisture content. As each type dries, put into a lidded container or a tightly closed polythene bag. Strip the leaves from their stalks, shred the larger ones, spread on box lids or trays and dry in the same way. Although sun-drying is the most natural and successful way, you can dry the materials in an airing cupboard, keeping a close watch on them and bringing them out when they become as crisp as cornflakes. In very windy weather this method is obviously preferable. Do not try to hasten the process by drying in front of direct artificial heat, such as an electric fire. This will draw the fragrance from the plants.

When all the petals, flowers and leaves have dried, put them in a large earthenware container with a lid or a large lidded polythene bowl. Sprinkle the salt between each layer, stir well, cover and leave for 2–3 weeks, stirring occasionally. Then stir in the powdered orris root, ground cinnamon, allspice, cloves and nutmeg, the thinly pared lemon and orange rind, finely chopped, and the shredded vanilla pod. Lastly add 1 teaspoon of flower oils or essence, or culinary essence, depending on what is available where you live. For a luxurious touch, add 1 teaspoon brandy. Cover the jar again, shake well and leave to mature for

a further 2–3 days. When the pot-pourri is ready, put it into glasses, brandy balloons, pretty teacups or bowls – Chinese porcelain bowls are traditional. If the pot-pourri dries out, as it is likely to do, particularly if left uncovered in a centrally-heated room, sprinkle on a little more salt, flower oil or essence and stir well. It should be kept constantly moist.

Dry pot-pourri

For the dry pot-pourri method, dry the petals, flowers and leaves as described and mix together with 100g (4oz) of powdered orris root, the fixative, and any of the spices suggested in the 'moist' recipe – or with your own choice. Put into a covered container and leave for two to three weeks, shaking frequently, before putting into jars, scent bottles or bowls or sewing into sachets, dolly bags or tiny pillows.

If you like the idea of preserving a single scent, use the dry method. You simply dry the flowers or leaves, add a little spice for muskiness and orris root powder, the preservative. A tangy geranium mixture is made with 2 handfuls each of rose-scented and lemon-scented geranium leaves. Snip off the stalks, dry the leaves in the sun or in an airing cupboard and crumble them gently in your hands so they break up but do not go to powder. Add 2 dessertspoons ground allspice, 1 teaspoon grated nutmeg and 1 ounce of powdered orris root and the mixture is complete.

To capture the scent of roses, take 4 handfuls of dried rose petals and 1 handful of dried mock orange blossom petals. Mix them together and add 2 ounces each of ground coriander seeds and powdered orris root and 1 dessertspoon of ground cinnamon. Mix well together.

FILOGRAPHY

Equipment

The equipment necessary for filography is listed below. It is simple and inexpensive.

Board. This should be at least 1.25cm ($\frac{1}{2}$in) thick when using short nails, and must not warp. Five to seven ply is ideal. When using 5cm (2in) nails, as in many of the circle designs, 2cm ($\frac{5}{8}$in) ply is correct. The supplier will cut to size, so a light rubbing with fine sandpaper is normally all you need to do. Avoid blockboard or chipboard as the odd nail can work loose, which could spoil the whole design.

Nails. For the flat designs 1.25cm ($\frac{1}{2}$in) panel or veneer pins should be used. Six millimetres ($\frac{1}{4}$in) of each nail should be left showing when you have hammered it into the board. For the circle designs 4 or 5cm ($1\frac{1}{2}$ or 2in) nails, preferably with fancy heads, are used. With these, 1.25cm ($\frac{1}{2}$in) is hammered into the board.

Accessories. You also need a fairly heavy hammer. Long, pointed pliers are used for holding each nail in position ready for the first tap. Small wire snippers are necessary if using wire. A bradawl is useful for marking the nail positions through the paper design. Some people find it useful to have a heavy metal strip 6mm ($\frac{1}{4}$in) thick and about 23cm (9in) long to

check the height of the nails when hammering a long row.

Drawing instruments. You need a collection of rulers showing various divisions, centimetres and inches. Two circular plastic protractors, one 13cm (5in) in diameter, and the other 10cm (4in) and a good supply of pencils are essential.

Thread. This is your choice. Both cotton and wool are possible, white or coloured. These are difficult to keep clean, and you may prefer to use nylon single-strand cord $\frac{1}{4}$mm in circumference. Drums of this can be purchased in shops dealing with window display supplies.

Copper or steel wire. This is available from ex-Army stores and junk shops. Buy old flex where the rubber is rotten, and comes off easily. Check that it is perfectly clean, and always lacquer it immediately you strip off the outer covering in order to prevent discoloration.

Paint. The board is painted after the nails have been placed in position. A matt black spray gives the best results and shows cotton, metal and nylon to advantage. If you use a brush, matt blackboard paint is used, but be careful not to let the paint clog between the nails. You can choose any colour you like, but always keep a good contrast between the board colour and the thread or

Filography produces some wide ranging results, from geometric abstracts to highly representational work like the picture above. Colour gives added flexibility.

135

wire. A spray paint leaves a pleasant, smooth finish, which is difficult to obtain using a brush. An undercoat may also be necessary.

Basic method

Preparing the board

First, choose the design that appeals and then draw it carefully to scale on a sheet of paper which is large enough to wrap round the sides of your board. The grid squares in the diagrams will help to reproduce accurately the lines and angles of the design as you enlarge it.

In each case, a suitable scale for the enlargement of the design is suggested, and the number of nails is specified for this size.

You can, of course, vary the size if you wish, depending on your board (remember that it is desirable to leave a margin of a few centimetres around the design). But if you do not use the suggested scale, you may need more or fewer nails to the line: the closer the nails, the better the result, but it is not practical to have them closer than 2.5mm ($\frac{1}{10}$in). So you will need to work out your optimum number of nails by taking the shortest line and seeing how many will comfortably fit into it. For example, if your shortest line is 9cm, and you want your nails 3mm apart, you would work it out as follows, in millimetres: $90 \div 3 = 30$ $+1 = 31$.

(You add one because, obviously, the number of nails is always one more than the number of spaces between them.)

Having established 31 as your number of nails, see how far apart these should be in the larger lines. Suppose you have a line of 18cm: $180 \div 30$ (not 31!) $= 6$. So your nails will be 6mm apart in this line.

Now, using a ruler or protractor, and a sharp pencil, mark on your paper each nail position. Place the drawing on the sandpapered board, wrap the sides around the edges of the board and fix with strips of Sellotape at the back. Using a bradawl or metal spike, punch a hole through the paper into the board for each nail. Remove the drawing and, by placing the ruler alongside each row of holes, check that all are perfectly straight and the same distance apart.

Using long, pointed pliers, guide each nail into each dent and tap with the hammer; remove pliers and hammer to the correct depth. If in doubt, place a metal bar 6mm ($\frac{1}{4}$in) thick alongside, so that you can see exactly how much of the nail is protruding. If a nail is not in far enough, a tap will do, but if you have hammered a nail in too far, the best way is to remove it carefully with pliers, placing a small piece of cardboard on the board where the pliers would touch so you do not mark it during the removal. Then, using a longer nail, hammer it into the hole. This is the main reason why you should choose a thicker board than you apparently need.

To straighten the nails in a row, lightly tap with a hammer, and to straighten a nail that is leaning at an angle towards the next one, place the blade of a screwdriver between them, and straighten with a light tap on the end of the screwdriver shaft.

When all the nails are in position, spray with paint. With transparent nylon thread matt black is probably best, but you may prefer some other contrast: a dark purple can give a most interesting effect. Remember that once you start weaving you will not be able to touch up the paint, so spray at least two coats, and check that the edges are not missed – paint is rapidly absorbed and you might find you have to paint the edge with

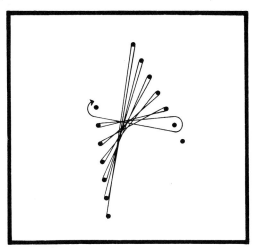

The thread should be kept taut.

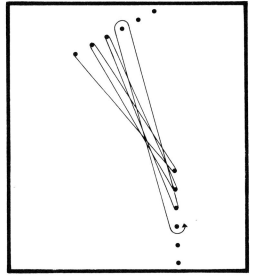

Always take it in same direction.

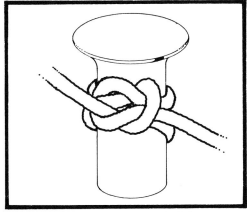

A simple left over right and right over left knot.

a brush. Be careful not to use too much paint, as a surplus easily clogs at the base of the nails. This is almost bound to occur if you use a brush, nor will you achieve that lovely silky finish that is obtained with a spray; so this is one time when it is worth spending a little more and using the spray. If the wood is porous, spray on an undercoat primer first.

Weaving

When the board is completely dry, you are ready to start weaving, using copper or steel flex wire or single nylon thread. (Coloured wool or white cotton give pleasant results, but in damp weather they are inclined to sag and may slip off the nails.)

Using nylon thread, start and finish with a reef knot. Keep the thread taut all the time, as even nylon threads expand under damp conditions. This tautness is particularly important when the threads stretch over 30cm (12in) between the nails, and in this case it is best to twist the thread twice round each nail to make it doubly secure.

In the great majority of diagrams, rows of nails will be represented by lines, each marked by a letter of the alphabet. The position of the first and last nails will be marked by the relevant figures; the others can then be inserted at equidistant intervals, once you have worked out their position. Thus each nail can be identified by a combination of letter and number, e.g. B2, C13, H6, etc.

The weaving instructions outline in detail the first few moves of any sequence until the pattern of the sequence is clear. It is then easy to continue the pattern in a sequential manner until the final point is reached as stated in the instructions. It is important to take the thread round each nail in the same direction.

Elementary designs

These three pages show three easy designs to help you begin filography.

DESIGN 1

This is a very striking design which shows that the simple shape can often be just as effective as the more complicated ones. You can look at it horizontally or vertically.

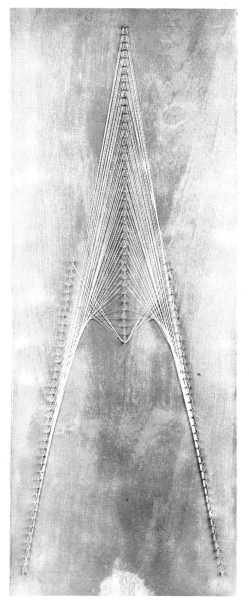

Scale
1 square = 2.5cm (1in).

Method
C41–B1–A41–A40–B2–C40–C39–B3–A39–A38–B4–C38, etc. to C1.

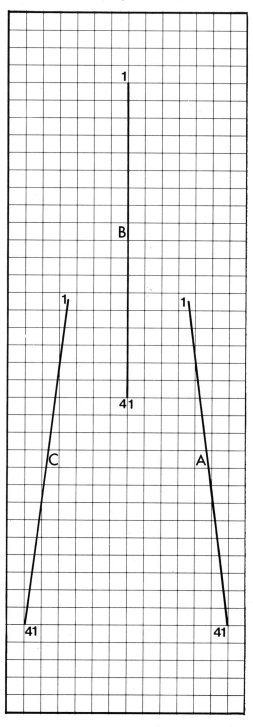

DESIGN 2

This abstract design should be drawn carefully on paper first, and by changing the angles and lengths of the lines, new designs can be evolved.

Scale

1 square = 2.5cm (1in).

Method

B1–A1–C1–B2–A2–C2, etc. to C31.

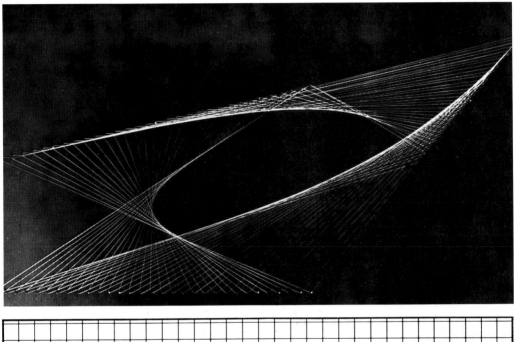

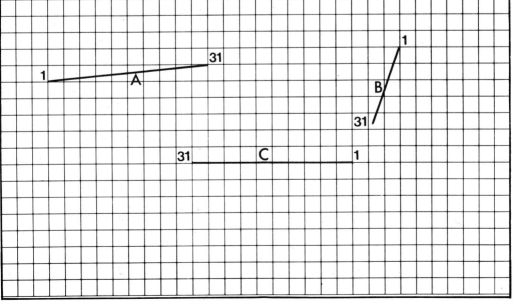

DESIGN 3

This stylised design represents the Eiffel Tower with a seagull on either side. The effect is one of geometric elegance.

Scale

1 square = 2.5cm (1in).

Method

These instructions raise a point of technique. When moving from one nail to an adjacent nail in the same row (e.g. A1–A2), you should execute an 'S' shape with the thread, bringing it round to the front of the second nail as shown. This ensures that the thread lies on the same side of each nail, so that the distance between the threads is constant all the way along the row.

Seagulls

A5–C1–B5–C1–A4–C2–B4–C2, etc. to B1.

Tower

D1–E1–F1–G1–H1–H2–G2–F2–E2–D2–D3. etc. to H41.

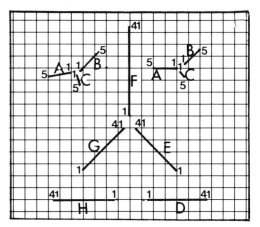

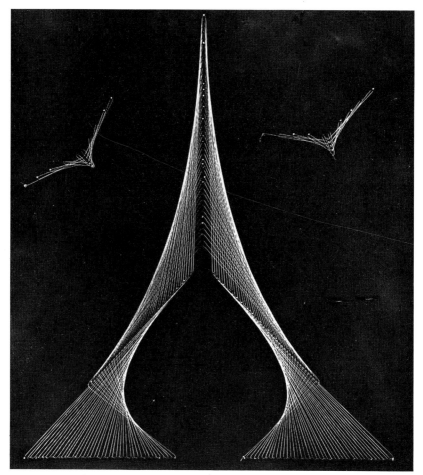

Circles

First prepare your template. Use a sheet of plain paper the size of the board and on this draw your circle in pencil. Mark a dot at the exact centre of the circle, place a circular plastic protractor on this, and make a small mark on the edge against each ten-degree division. This gives you the thirty-six points.

Now, using a ruler, carefully extend these thirty-six marks to cut the edge of the circle, thus giving the actual nail positions.

Sellotape the paper onto the board, and pierce each nail position with a bradawl. Most designs call for 5cm (2in) nails, of which 1.25cm ($\frac{1}{2}$in) is hammered into the board.

After painting comes the threading operation. If, however, you decide to glue a sheet of copper over the board to act as the background, this should be glued with Araldite, following the instructions, naturally making sure the board is the correct size first. The template is Sellotaped over this, and the nail positions marked with a bradawl, as before. This procedure is also followed if using a formica-faced board. Very carefully hand-drill each nail hole after removing the paper. If using an electric drill, make sure you pierce only the metal, as a deeper hole will result in loose nails. Be very careful not to scratch the metal surface and protect it when using the hammer, as a bad shot will result in an unsightly dent. The metal should, of course, have been lacquered in the first place to prevent future discoloration.

Using wire or nylon thread, choose any nail and secure the thread with a reef knot. Following Fig 1 count eleven nails, lay your thread around the outside of the nail, pull taut, count to the next eleventh nail, and repeat until every nail in the circle

has been used once. If you arrive at a nail that has already been used, stretch the thread outside the edge of the circle to the next unused nail, and continue.

It is important that every thread in the pattern is the same length and at the same angle, or the final pattern will be ruined. When all thirty-six nails have been used, you should find that the thread has arrived back at the nail from which you started. Repeat the process exactly, constructing a second layer over the first. Then repeat again until you have six similar layers. Keep pressing the thread to the base of each nail.

Now weave another six layers, but counting to every ninth nail. Then weave another six layers using every seventh nail, fifth and, finally, every third nail. If you notice that the thickness of each six layers is taking more or less than a sixth of the height of the nails, you should vary the number of layers, as the aim is to have the nails completely full when the design is complete. Tie a neat reef knot to finish.

Using a new length of thread, tie it to any nail, and run it round and round the outside of the circle, rather like

the outside of a drum, until you have filled in the height of the nails. This is a neat finish, and hides the knots. The weaving in this example is 3.75cm (1½in) deep. Naturally, if you use 15 or 20cm (6 to 8in) nails a very interesting cone shape can be achieved. A further suggestion would be to use dark-coloured threads at the base of the cone, and gradually lighten the shade as the work proceeds. You could also add to the effect by gluing a circular mirror inside the circle of nails at the start.

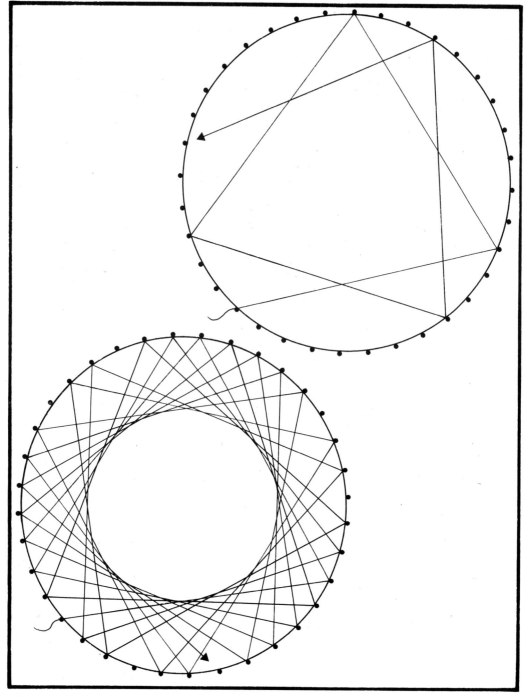

DESIGN 4

When you have mastered the circle, it can be incorporated into many designs. This one is done on teak with steel wire.

Scale
1 square = 2.5cm (1in).

Method
A1 – B1 – C1 – D1 – A1 – A2 – B2 – C2 – D2 – A2, etc., to . . . A6–B6–C6–D6–A6. Work the circle as on previous page.

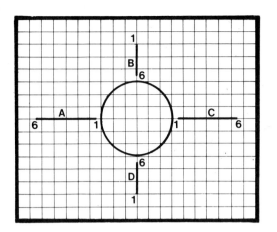

Star

Scale
1 square = 2.5cm (1in).

Method
A1 – B1 – C1 – D1 – E1 – F1 – G1 – H1 – J1 –
K1 – L1 – M1 – N1 – O1 – P1 – Q1 – A2,
etc., to Q43–A43, A1–C43–E1–G43–J1
–L43–N1–P43–A2, etc., to P1–A43.

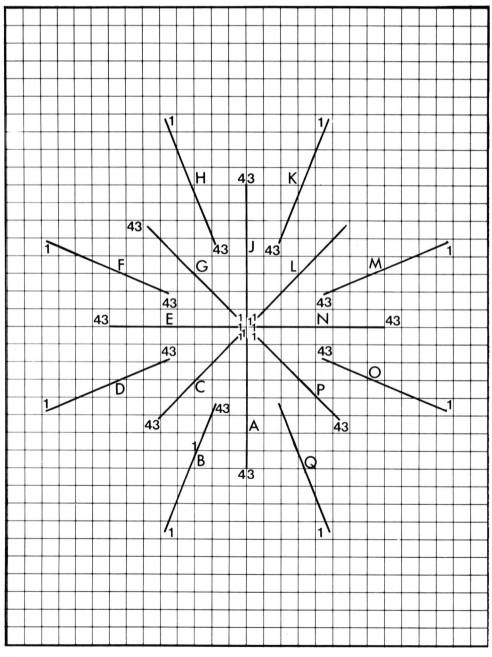

*This delicate star shows off
especially well the graceful lines
that can be obtained in filography.*

Windmill sails

Diagram shows one spoke of the windmill.

Scale
1 square = 1.25cm ($\frac{1}{2}$in).

Centre angles
$\frac{360}{7} = 51\frac{3}{7}$ degrees

Method
B1–A16–B2–A15–B3–A14, etc., to A1, then A16–D1–C16–D2–C15–D3, etc., to C1–C16–F1, etc. Continue thus for each sail.

The result will be neater if one nail only is used in the centre – to do duty for B1, D1, F1, H1, K1, M1 and O1.

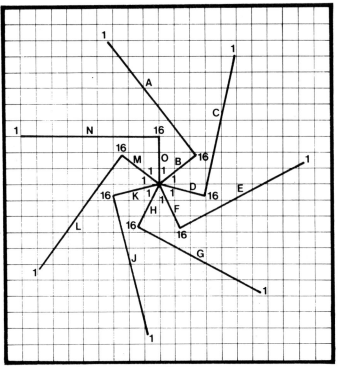

Position nails as shown in diagram above.

For best results in this design,
the threads should radiate
literally from one central nail.

Tudor rose

This seemingly complex design breaks down into a 36-nail circle with the two basic shapes shown in Fig 13; these two shapes are used five times to surround the circumference of the circle and then, slightly larger, another five times round the outside of the design (see Fig 13 for the way in which the larger set fits round the smaller; you should use this figure to construct your own design to scale). The weaving instructions are for the two basic shapes and are simply repeated for each of the ten sections making up the complete figure.

The Tudor rose shown here is on a 60cm (2ft) square board.

Method

A1–B16–C1–D16–D15–C2–B15–A2–A3, etc., to A16.

K1–L1–M1–M2–L2–K2–K3, etc., to K16.

Circle

1st layer, every 15th nail.
2nd layer, every 11th nail.
3rd layer, every 7th nail.

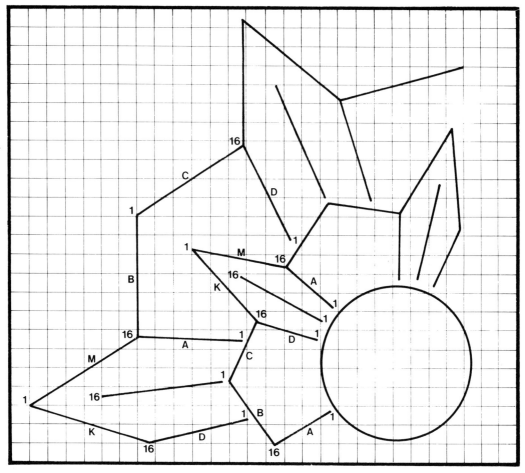

*The petals of the Tudor Rose
look complex but only involve
the repetition of two basic shapes.*

Sailing ship

This sailing ship was constructed on a formica-covered board, and the outline of the hull is a length of copper wire, lacquered. Great care must be taken to prevent the formica from splitting when hammering in the nails; lightly tap a sharp bradawl into each nail position first.

This is an example where one series of nylon strands overlaps another series of nails, and care must be taken that they are evenly spaced as they pass between the nails. Use a double-size nail at the top of the mast to take the strain of the twenty-odd strands.

Scale

1 square = 1.25cm ($\frac{1}{2}$in).

Method

A1-D1-A2-D1-A3-D1, etc., to A21.
B22-C1-B23-C2, etc., to B62-C41.
E1-D1-E2-D2, etc., to E38-D38.
B41-D1-B40-D2 etc., to B1-D41.

This design was worked on Formica.

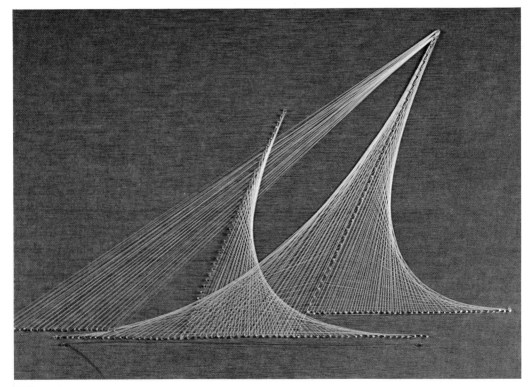

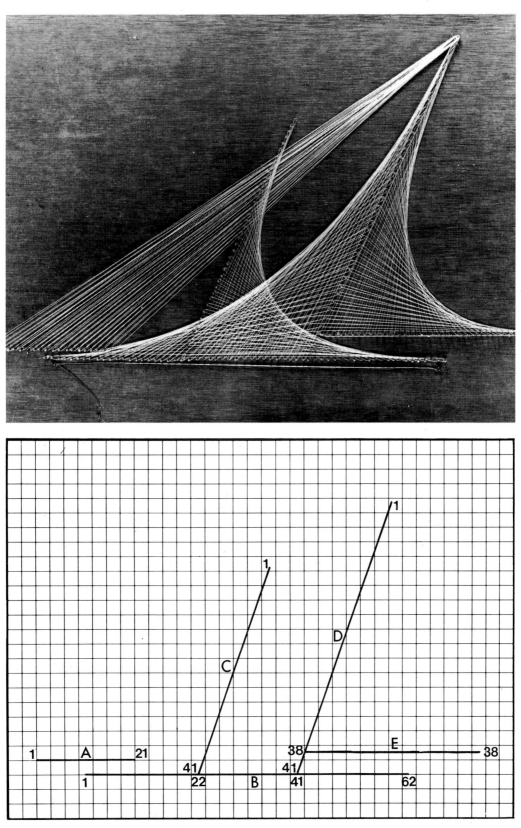

*An abstract design which
is not entirely symmetrical.*

An abstract

Scale

1 square = 1.25cm ($\frac{1}{2}$in).

Method

A1–B1–C1–D1–E1–F29–G1–H29–J1–
K29–A2, etc., to K1–A29.
F29 – N1 – F28 – N2 – F27 – N3, etc., to
N29.
M1–A29–L1–M2–A28–L2–M3, etc., to
L29.

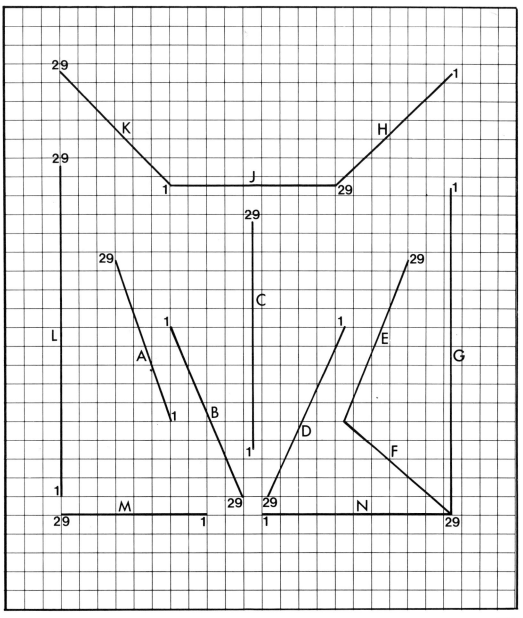

MACRAMÉ

Equipment

The basic tools for macramé work are simple and consist of scissors, glass-headed pins, and a knotting board. All other items are accessories or adornments. The embroidery needle and crochet hook are used occasionally for finishing off. Chopsticks, hardwood, beads, rings, and loops for headings and decorations are also used.

The knotting board. This is the working surface. The most suitable material for this is a piece of insulating board, or cork, covered with brown paper. The board must be lightweight and rigid but soft enough for pins to be inserted easily.

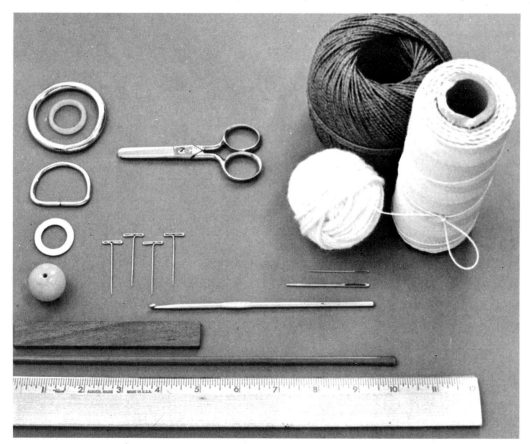

Basic macramé equipment is shown above, plus the beads, rings and woodstrips usually required for adornment.

Yarns. Yarns used for macramé should be strong enough to withstand the abrasion that knotting produces, and should not have a lot of give or elasticity. Smooth-surfaced yarns are best since they are the most satisfactory to work with and do not detract from the textural interest of the knots.

The most widely used yarns are: Macramé twine, sisal, jute, crochet cotton, Seine twine, Filler cord, Lurex cord, rug wool and parcel string.

Knitting yarns are not desirable since they have too much elasticity, but some, e.g., Aran wools, can be used once their limitations are understood and samples have been made with them.

The term 'thread' is used here to mean a yarn other than wool. The illustrations show the relative thicknesses and texture of the yarns. From these readers are encouraged to make their own choice of thread and colours.

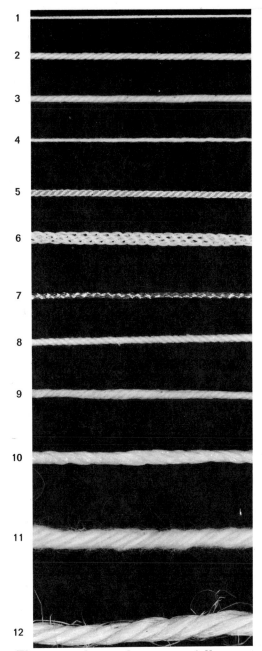

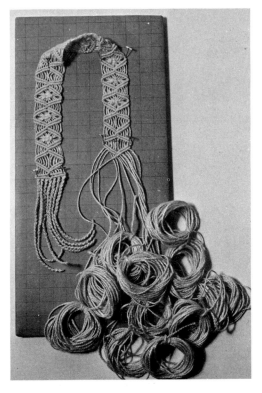

The yarns shown above are as follows:
1. Strutts super glace 2. Strutts glace
3. 'Needlewoman' Macramé twine
4. Filler cord 5. Nylon Seine twine
6. Novacord 7. Lurex cord 8. Piping cord 9. Parcel string 10. Broplene twine
11. Turkey rug wool 12. 4-ply sisal.

A knotting board (left) must be rigid but take pins easily.

155

Preparing the yarn

The yarn is prepared for knotting by calculating the length of the ends and measuring off. An end is an individual length of yarn.

How to calculate. The ends should be 3½ to 4 times longer than the piece you plan to make, but since they are doubled in half for knotting, they are measured 7 to 8 times longer. For example, if the piece will have a finished length of 0.9m (1yd), measure each end to 6.4m or 7.3m (7 or 8yd). When each end is doubled for knotting, it will then be two ends, each 3.1m to 3.6m (3½ to 4yd) long. Measure ends generously and then add to them. It is better to have extra yarn than to run short and have to add at an inconvenient place in the design.

Making a sample. Heavy yarns take up more length in knotting than lightweight ones, so allow for this in the calculations. Make a sample, at least 76mm × 152mm (3in × 6in) to gauge the length and to see how many ends will be needed for the width. To determine the number, tie four ends into a Flat Knot (overleaf) and measure the knot's width. If it is 12mm (½in) for example, you know

you will need eight ends to the inch. When you know what you want to make, or if you are searching for ideas, knot the yarn in several ways to know how it will tie and to gauge its texture and desirability.

Keep notes of the amount used, its source, the number of ends and their length. Such records are valuable when planning future macramé pieces.

Measuring off ends
Warping board. Once you know how long the ends should be, measure them off. This can be done with a 0.5m × 0.9m (½yd × 1yd) weaver's warping board. Begin by cutting one end, in a contrasting colour, to the calculated length.

Following Fig 1, tie this measuring cord around peg A and wind it out to its full length as shown in the diagram. Making a cross between pegs G and H keeps the ends in order. With the measuring cord as guide, measure off the ends and cut them at peg A.

In this way, ends may be removed in sections, and measurements will not be lost.

To keep easier count of the ends, tie every group of ten with a loose loop of contrasting yarn.

Other methods. If you don't have a warping board, C-clamps, or holding pegs, can be used. Attach clamps to opposite ends of a table and wind the yarn from peg to peg. Remember to make the cross. There is still another method. It takes longer, but it works. Measure the yarn against

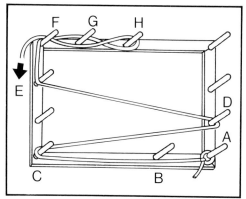

1. Measure off ends on warping board.

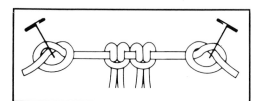

2. Mount ends on holding card.

a yardstick, then cut it. Keeping this end as the measuring cord, measure off the needed number of ends.

Method

Knotting board. The board is covered with brown wrapping paper, which affords good contrast to the yarns. Pull the paper tightly over the board, tape it on the reverse side, and mark it off into 25mm (1in) squares. These guidelines will help you knot to the correct length and width.

A convenient point to begin the work is usually the middle of the board, or about 254mm (10in) from the bottom. As knotting progresses, move the work upwards.

Holding cord. The ends are knotted onto a holding cord (a horizontal length) with the Reversed Cording Knot (see Fig 2) or onto a chop stick, ring, bracelet or whatever you feel suits the piece. They can also be looped around the pins. Tie an Overhand Knot on each side of the holding cord and pin securely to the knotting board (see Fig 2). The cord must be kept taut. At times it is also used as a knot-bearing cord (over which knots are tied); in that case, make an Overhand Knot on one side only, preferably the left.

As each end is knotted onto the holding cord, pin it to the board. Move pins down constantly as the work progresses. They should never be more than 25mm (1in) from the working area and can even be just in the row above. Slant pins away from you, and anchor them firmly. If the design should become irregular, either the pinning is not sufficient or some knots are being tied too tightly.

Winding ends
When ends are too long to handle

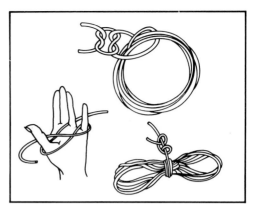

3. Two simple ways of reducing inconveniently long ends.

conveniently, their lengths can be reduced by making hand bobbins or butterflies (see Fig 3), or by using rubber bands. Each end is wound separately.

General hints
1. Keep the holding cord in a steady position when mounting ends.
2. Keep the knot-bearing cord motionless and taut when in use.
3. Tie every knot close to the previous knot unless directed otherwise.
4. Keep ends straight, in order, and not twisted, particularly when knots are being made over them.
5. Ends are always doubled in half before knotting begins. When the number of cut ends is given in the projects, this always refers to measured-off ends and not to doubled ends.

Knots
Only two elementary knots are essential to macramé - the Half Knot, also called the Macramé Knot, and the Half Hitch. There are various combinations of these knots.
Knots can be easily learned from the diagrams given here. Practise them by making samples, using different yarns and doubling the number of ends. Make the knots in light-coloured yarns so they can be seen.

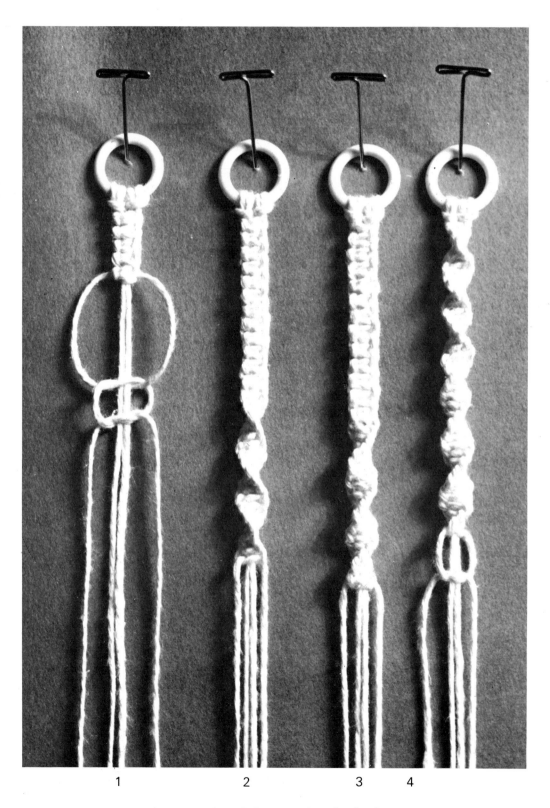

1   2   3   4

A progression of sinnets using the flat knot,
reversed flat knot and the half knot.

The Flat Knot and the Half Knot

The Flat Knot is made up of two Half Knots, one going to the left, the other to the right. Four ends are used; the centre two, known as fillers or core ends, are held taut until the knot is completed. As you practise you will be making sinnets (braided cording) shown opposite.

The knotting patterns in the photograph correspond by number with those used in the sinnet illustrated. In Sinnet No. 1 the knotting pattern consists of a series of Flat Knots. In 2 and 3, a Flat Knot alternates with a Reversed Flat Knot. A twist is obtained by repeating Half Knots. 4 combines lower 2 and 3.

How to make the sinnets on the opposite page.

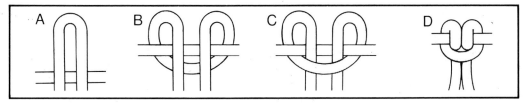

How to mount ends on holding cord with Reversed Cording.

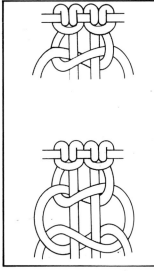

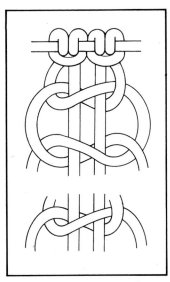

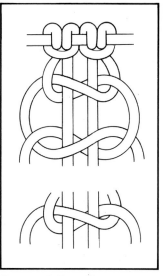

Half Knot (top) and completed Flat Knot.

Flat Knot with Half Knot twist.

Reversed Flat Knot and Half Knot twist.

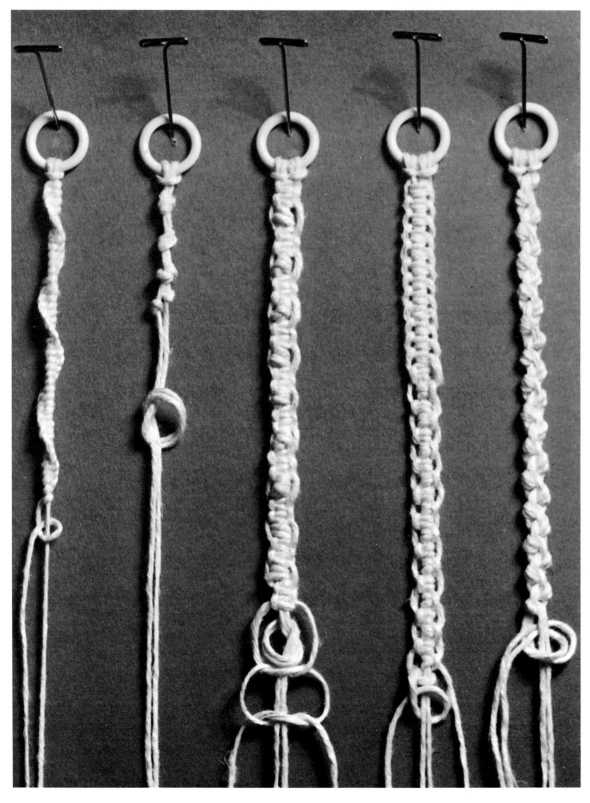

Half Hitch and Overhand Knot

The Half Hitch is the most practical knot in macramé since a number of variations may be obtained from it. The Overhand Knot is tied in a way somewhat similar to the Half Hitch but is applied differently. A series of Overhand Knots using either a single end or multi-ends creates texture. It also can be used to end a sinnet, or it can be used between Flat Knots to give interest to the design.

Both knots are shown, figs 5 and 6.

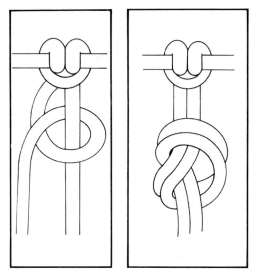

5. Half Hitch Knot. Continue for sinnet.
6. Overhand Knot using two ends.

To make 7.   To make 8.   To make 9.

Cording

It would be difficult to say which of the Cording variations gives the most exciting results. They are certainly all distinctive. Three versions are diagrammed here – the Horizontal, Vertical, and Diagonal. Each end goes over the knot-bearing cord twice while completing the row (making two Half Hitches). Keep the knot-bearer secure across each row and held sharply in the determined direction. Draw up knots closely and pin each row after completion. The knot-bearer must be measured off longer than other ends. All three variations can be used together.

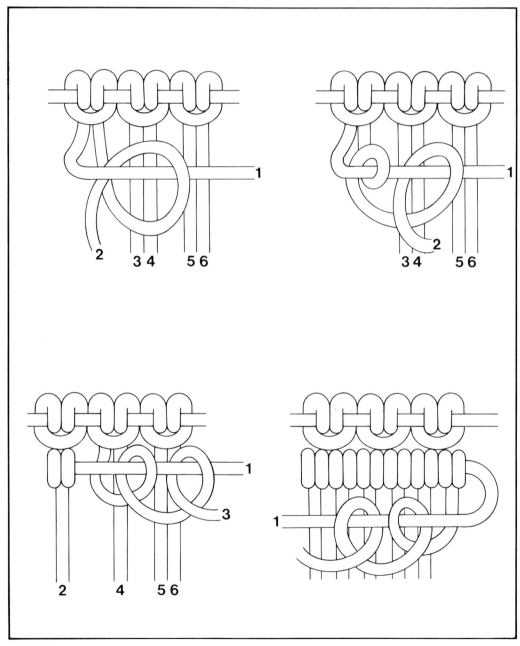

To make horizontal rows, follow diagrams from left to right.

162

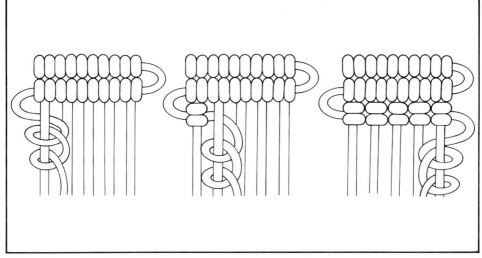

Three diagrams showing how to make vertical cording.

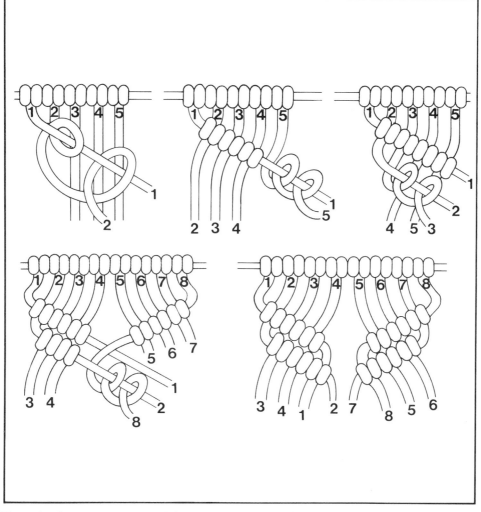

To make diagonal cording, follow diagrams from left to right.

Headings and picots

There are various ways of mounting ends onto a holding cord and some are very decorative indeed.

The picots shown are looped knots used to give variation to edge headings and other areas where a lacy effect is desired to add interest to the project.

Reversed cording.

Double cording.

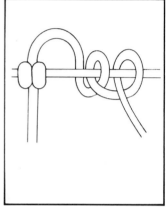

Double cording, picot.

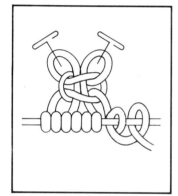

Flat knots, picots.

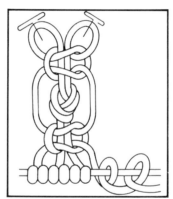

Variation on a theme.

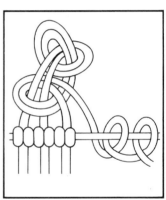

Double chain knot.

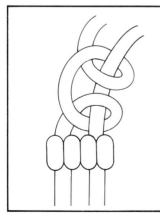

Combination cording.

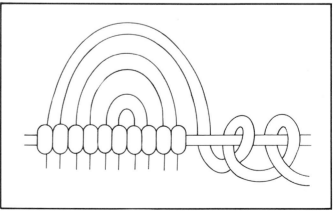

A series of different kinds of picots.

Finishing

For finishing off a piece, the remaining ends can be worked into a decorative fringe, or formed into sinnets, or they can be neatly trimmed, making a simple fringed edge. A Gathering Knot can be made using as many ends as you want. Tie it tightly so that it will hold and give a crisp look to the work. The ends can also be woven into the reverse side with an embroidery needle or crochet hook. Still another way is to set in a holding cord and mount a single row of Cording, followed by a Flat Knot and sinnets ending with a Gathering Knot.

Splicing can be done when ends have broken or need to be extended. Overlap ends and continue knotting to work them in (see diagrams below).

Decorative edgings. Flat Knots with multi-ends and Overhand Knots can be used to make decorative edges on curtains or tablecloths.

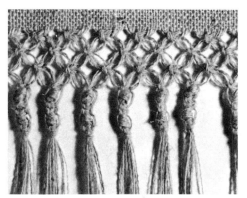

Hessian fringe made in Flat Knots using twelve ends.

Decoration with flat knots and picots.

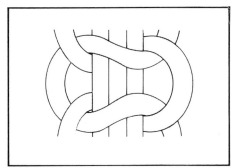

Splicing method for flat knot.

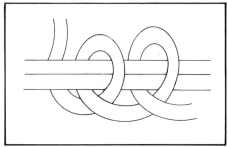

Splicing method for Cording.

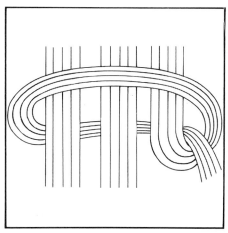

A crisp finish with a gathering knot.

165

Shopping bag

This project results in a handy and attractive piece and serves to introduce the Flat Knot used double and in an alternating technique. It is important here that the knots be kept evenly spaced.

Size

380mm (15in) wide at the centre, 610mm (25in) long, including bracelets and fringe.

Materials

Pink and green thread. This tying cord is available where gift wrappings are sold.

Two bracelets. If you can get matching coloured bracelets, do so; then they will not have to be covered with knots.

Knots

Half Hitch. Reversed Cording. Flat and Double Flat in alternating rows.

Cut ends

Pink – 18 ends, each 3.66m (4yd) long. Green – 18 ends, each 3.66m (4yd) long.

2 extra ends, one of each colour, 0.9m (1yd) long each, to cover bracelets.

Method

Use a long narrow knotting board since it will be inserted between the

two sides of the piece. As you make each knot, dampen it with wet fingertips. Do not get knots too wet or the yarn fibres will separate.

Knot Half Hitches on bracelet.

To begin. Partially cover one bracelet with pink yarn, using the Half Hitch as shown. Attach 10 ends (that is, 5 doubled) of pink with the Reversed Cording. Attach 16 ends (8 doubled) of green in the same manner. Attach 10 more ends of pink in the same manner. Fill up remaining spaces with Half Hitches in pink. Repeat with second bracelet except reverse the colour order.

Using the edge of the knotting board as shown, bring the two sides of the shopping bag together.

Work each side as follows. 2 rows Flat Knots alternating. Knot them close together. 1 row of Double Flat Knots alternating (see diagram). Leave 10mm ($\frac{3}{4}$in) space and do a 2nd row of Double Flat Knots alternating. Leave 25mm (1in) space and do a 3rd row of Double Flat Knots alternating. Pin the two sides next to each other and on each side do 3 more rows of Double Flat Knots alternating.

Now join the sides together as shown in the photograph, using the edges of the knotting board. From this point on the piece lies on both sides of the board. Continue knotting to the length of the bag.

To finish. When you have worked all the knots down to the same point, match the two sides knot for knot. Tie bundles of 8 ends together, using an Overhand Knot and leave 50mm (2in) hanging. Or turn the bag inside out, tie an Overhand Knot on the inside, and trim excess close to the knot.

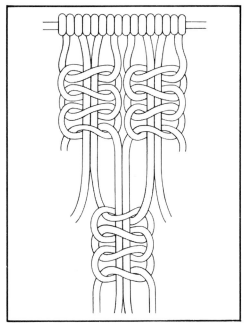

Double Flat Knots in alternating rows.

Flat Knots alternating.

Holder with picots.

Hanging pot plant holders

The two projects shown here use sinnets and few knots. They are designed to help you create charming and useful pieces by combining yarn and found objects. The general rule that ends should measure $3\frac{1}{2}$ to 4 times the finished length of the piece does not apply since there are so few knots to tie.

Holder for dried grasses

Materials
Twine.
Any cylindrical- or conical-shape.
A disc with four holes or a ring is used for the base.

Knots
Flat, Reversed Cording, Overhand.

Cut ends
8 ends, each 2.4m ($2\frac{3}{4}$yd) long.

Method
Following Fig. 1, into each hole of the base, or at four places on a ring, mount two ends, using the Reversed Cording. This gives four ends from each hole. Make a Flat Knot with each four ends. Take two ends from each knot; leave 32mm ($1\frac{1}{4}$in) space. Tie a Flat Knot, Overhand Knot, and Flat Knot. Take two ends from each knot; leave 50mm (2in) space. With outside ends of each Flat Knot, tie an Overhand Knot with four ends.

To finish. Tie the ends together with an Overhand Knot and trim.

Hanging vase

Materials
Twine.
The container is a triangular jam jar.

Knots
Flat, Overhand, Picot.

Cut ends
6 ends, each 2.7m (3yd) long.

Method
Following Fig. 2 below, intertwine four ends with the loop ends. With each four ends, make a sinnet of 5 Flat Knots. *Take the two outside ends and leave 25mm (1in) space. Make an Overhand Knot. Bring one core end each from 2 Square Knots and make a Flat Knot below the Overhand Knot. Next make 3 Picot Knots (page 164), ending with 1 Flat Knot*. Repeat * to * with the other ends. Take two ends from each knot, leave 50mm (2in) space, and tie an Overhand Knot with four ends. Do 2 more such knots with the other ends.

To finish. About 711mm (28in) from the last knot, gather the ends together and make an Overhand Knot by which to hang the piece.

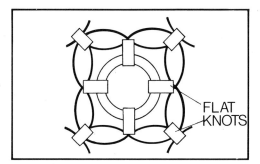

1. Base of dried grasses holder.

2. To start hanging vase base.

A sash

This vivid three-coloured sash, in a repeat diagonal design, is achieved primarily with the Diagonal Cording Knot worked in a closely knotted pattern on both sides. An additional feature of this sash is the decorative use of the bobble.

This sash may be made as long as you wish by repeating the pattern.

Materials
Orange thread.
Rug wool.
Rose and black.

Knots
Diagonal Cording, Flat Knot, Overhand Knot, and Bobble.

Width
Rose and orange: 4 ends each.
Black: 2 ends.

Method
Arrange ends as follows, pinning each loop: 2 black, 4 rose, 8 orange, 4 rose, 2 black.
Leave 356m (14in) free before beginning to knot.

For beginning section. With outside black end do Diagonal Cording to centre. Repeat with black end on other side.
Cross the two ends where they meet and continue in this manner for 3 rows, which brings four ends in rose to middle.

Multicolour sash with bobbles which is worked on both sides with Diagonal Cording.

Make a bobble with the four centre ends in rose, using 5 Flat Knots (see diagram).

Continue with the Diagonal Cording for 8 more rows. (This brings the four black ends to the middle.)

Make a bobble, using 5 Flat Knots.

Turn piece over. Continue with

Diagonal Cording for 8 rows.

Turn piece over. Make an orange bobble.

Pattern repeat. *Turn piece over. Do 10 rows Diagonal Cording.*

Continue * to * until centre section is of desired length.
Be sure to turn piece every 10 rows.

For ending section. Make an orange bobble. Turn piece over and do 6 rows Diagonal Cording.
Turn piece over and make a rose bobble.
Turn piece over and do 4 rows Diagonal Cording.
Turn piece to front and do 2 rows Diagonal Cording.

Make a black bobble. Continue with Diagonal Cording until there are 10 rows in all.

To finish. Make Flat Knot sinnets with remaining ends and tie them with a Gathering Knot.

Making a bobble

Bobbles can be made to any size by changing the length of the Flat Knot sinnet. They can also be made with multi-end Flat Knots.

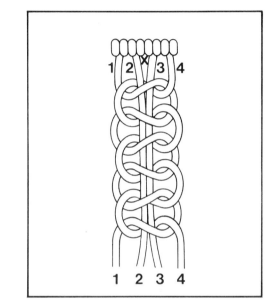

With three or more Flat Knots make a sinnet. Bring core ends up to beginning of sinnet between ends 2 and 3 (marked X), using crochet hook if necessary. Pull core ends down firmly and continue with the pattern.

A placemat

The Flat Knot used in alternating rows is the featured knot in this project, as it was in the shopping bag, but here it is more closely tied, giving a totally different effect. The knot-bearing cord, worked into the edge Flat Knots so that no loose ends will be exposed, is an example of how to do an expert job.

Size
330mm × 508mm (13in × 20in).

Material
Orange thread.

Knots
Flat Knot and Cording.

Cut ends
52 ends, each 5.1m (5yd 20in) long.

Holding Cord
3.6m (4yd).

Method
The holding cord is also the knot-bearing cord and is incorporated into the edge Flat Knot after being used for a row of Horizontal Cording, and all along the edge until needed again as a knot-bearing cord for the next row of Horizontal Cording. This will give three core ends, as shown.

To begin. Tie an Overhand Knot about 26mm (1in) in on the holding cord. Pin the knot securely to the board just before the beginning of a square and on a horizontal guideline. Using all the ends, do 1 row of Horizontal Cording (described previously). Return and do another row of Horizontal Cording.

Work as follows.
1 row – Double Flat Knots
1 row – Horizontal Cording
3 rows – Flat Knots alternating
1 row – Horizontal Cording
1 row – Triple Flat Knots (sinnets)
1 row – Horizontal Cording
5 rows – Flat Knots alternating
1 row – Horizontal Cording
*7 rows – Flat Knots alternating
1 row – Horizontal Cording*
Repeat * to * seven times
1 row – Horizontal Cording
5 rows – Flat Knots alternating
1 row – Horizontal Cording
3 rows – Flat Knots
1 row – Horizontal Cording
3 rows – Flat Knots alternating
1 row – Horizontal Cording
2 rows – Flat Knots
2 rows – Horizontal Cording

To finish. With an embroidery needle or crochet hook, weave in the ends on the back side for at least 12mm ($\frac{1}{2}$in). Trim. If the mat does not lay flat, pin it to size on the knotting board every 12mm ($\frac{1}{2}$in). Spray lightly with water and allow it to dry.

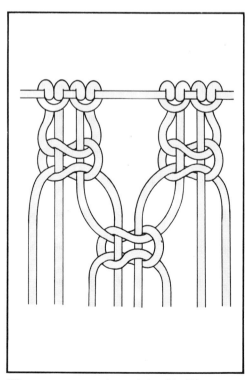

The pattern consists of double Flat Knots alternating.

172

Detail, showing variation of knots used in the mat.

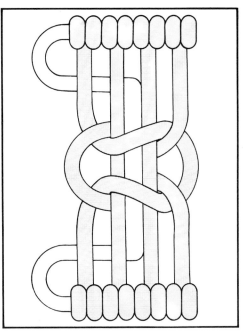

Flat Knot with three core ends. Third end is knot bearer and is worked into edge until needed.

SPECIAL TECHNIQUES

There are many creative projects that do not require unusual facilities or materials but can be made with things which are readily available. In this chapter several special techniques are explored – special in the sense that they require more imagination and ingenuity than expert knowledge or a large budget. For many of these projects the necessary materials can be found in an ordinary kitchen. Often a garden or nearby park or field can furnish both ideas and ingredients. For example, you could use different kinds of dried plants, or lentils or pasta, to make collages; projects which children would also enjoy. Apart from natural materials, the only other requirements are some mounting board and adhesive.

Pipecleaners, old or odd buttons, ribbon and leftover dress fabric are just a few of the sort of materials which are likely to be found in the home, and when combined with specially bought craft materials, a useful craft kit can be made.

Baby owl

This baby owl is an almost three-dimensional collage on a rough hessian backing (See also page 179.)

Materials
Brown feathery grass
for body.
Coarser brown grass
for wings.
Fluffy creamy-brown
grass-heads for chest.
Light feathery grass
above beak.
Honesty petals.
Straw-daisies
(helichrysums) for eyes.
Walnut-half for beak.
Chestnuts for feet.
Cork bark or thick twig.
Bay leaves or preserved
leaves.
A piece of heavy card,
56cm (22in) by 40cm (16in).
Unbleached hessian
the same size.

Owl made mostly of grass heads.

2m ($2\frac{1}{4}$yd) braid,
1.3cm ($\frac{1}{2}$in) wide, for frame.
Wallpaper paste.
Clear all-purpose adhesive.
Double-sided clear tape.
Strong adhesive tape.
1.3cm ($\frac{1}{2}$in) steel pins.
Adhesive tabs or rings
to hang.

Method

Trim the card evenly and make sure the corners are right-angles. Then spread thickly with wallpaper paste, and press the hessian down smoothly on top. When dry, bind each side with adhesive tape.

On a piece of paper at least 30cm (12in) deep by 22.8cm (9in) wide, rule a 7.6cm (3in) vertical line. With the point of your compasses at each end of the line, and a radius of 11.4cm ($4\frac{1}{2}$in), draw 22.8cm (9in) diameter semi-circles as in Fig 1 joining each side as indicated by the broken lines. Cut out and place this pattern on your hessian, 11.4cm ($4\frac{1}{2}$in) from the top, with 14cm ($5\frac{1}{2}$in) clear underneath and 7.6cm (3in) at each side. Draw round it.

Now begin to work out the composition of the owl. Four grass-heads of 15-to-20cm (6-to-8in) for each wing are used in the version illustrated. Stick on the wing grass-heads (beginning at the inside, and using clear all-purpose adhesive) so that the tops are hidden by the body grass. The grass heads are stuck down in sections, gradually making them smaller by breaking off just the amount needed to fill in the shape.

Begin at each side of the outline, working down towards the centre, and finishing across the top, with pieces going in both directions.

Mark a point 10cm (4in) below the top of his head for the beak.

Beginning at the lower edge of the chest, stick grass-heads in layers up to the level of the beak (following the illustration for the shape). Stick a tuft of grass-heads so that they will fan out above the beak.

To make up each eye, cut out a 7cm ($2\frac{3}{4}$in) diameter circle of tissue paper. Stick honesty petals (about eight) to the paper, overlapping each other and extending about 6mm ($\frac{1}{4}$in) over the outer edge of the circle (making the completed circle about 8.3cm ($3\frac{1}{4}$in) wide.

A good alternative eye is a dark wooden button, the centre picked out in natural raffia.

Stick the two circles at each side of the beak marking, about 12mm ($\frac{1}{2}$in) apart.

Beak. Now stick the beak into position, followed by a straw-daisy for each eye (anchor these with pins, hidden in the petals, if necessary).

Stick ears and feet into place (securing the latter with pins from the back. of the card).

Limb. Stick and pin the bark just below the owl's feet and arrange leaves above and below, fixing them in position with double-sided tape.

Finishing. If you want to stiffen the picture and add weight, tape another piece of card behind the first. Then stick braid round the edge and fix tabs or rings at the back to hang.

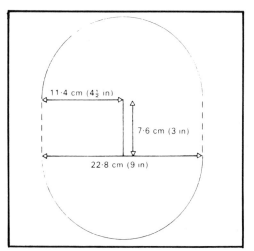

Dimensions of owl outline.

Corn dollies

In the United States, the European corn dolly tradition is perpetuated in attractive little figures made from the outer leaves of the ripe maize husk, with the 'silk' found inside the ear of corn used for hair.

Crêpe paper is a suitable alternative to maize for corn dollies, the grain and texture of the paper resembling the real thing very well. But you will have to colour it with poster paint.

To colour crêpe paper, dilute white poster colour in a saucer, then add a little colour at a time until you get a creamy-yellow shade, matching it to a skein of natural raffia.

Using a household paintbrush, slosh the wet paint onto white crêpe paper, working from side-to-side in lines *along* the grain of the paper. It is essential to use a good quality crêpe, otherwise it will disintegrate.

Hang the crêpe paper in a warm place to dry. The result will be rather stiff, uneven, and slightly crinkled – like sheets of home-grown maize!

Hair. Substitute stranded embroidery cotton for the hair 'silk' – choosing a darker shade than your paper.

Materials

White crêpe paper.
Poster paints (as described).
Natural raffia.
Matching cotton.
Stranded embroidery cotton.
Plasticine (white or stone).
Pipe cleaners.
Cotton wool.
Black ink or felt pen.
Fabric adhesive.
Household paintbrush.

Method

Colour the crêpe paper as described. Cut a piece of crêpe 25cm (10in) deep by 15cm (6in) wide for the body (see Fig 1 – arrows indicate direction of grain). Gather this neatly across the centre with the finger-tips (as indicated by broken line) and tie tightly with cotton. Fold in half (Fig 2).

Roll some plasticine into a ball the size of a large marble. Insert this between the folded paper, close under the tied centre, and smooth the paper round so that it leaves a flat area on one side for the face: tie tightly underneath (Fig 3).

Cut a piece of crêpe for the arms 10cm (4in) deep by 15cm (6in) wide (grain running across – see Fig 4), and then roll the paper loosely round it, tying tightly with cotton 1cm ($\frac{3}{8}$in) from each end: trim cut ends and tie a narrow strip of raffia round each wrist, over the cotton (Fig 5). Place the arms between the body, close under the neck, and tie tightly underneath (Fig 6).

Cut the skirt 15cm (6in) deep by 30cm (12in) wide (Fig 7). Fold in half *across* the grain (broken line): then open out flat again. Thread a needle with double cotton and gather along the fold line: fold again, then draw up gathers as tightly as possible and secure. Fit round the waist, join ends at the back, and then drive the needle through the body and back again, catching front of skirt to waist as

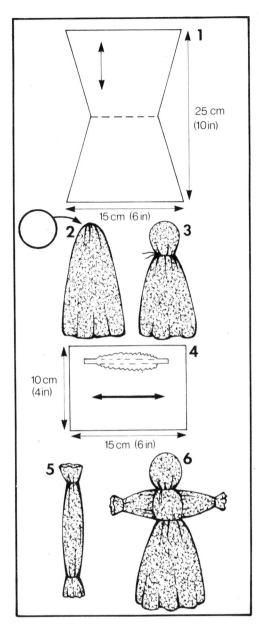

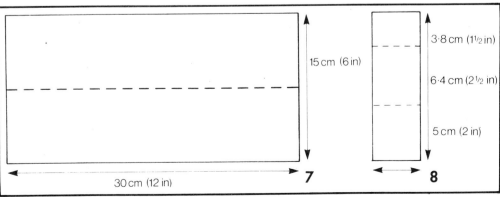

you do so. Trim lower edge if necessary, so that the figure stands steadily.

Cut the apron 15cm (6in) deep by 5cm (2in) wide. The broken lines in Fig 8 (previous page) indicate folds: fold the lower 5cm (2in) up and then stick the edge of the top 3.8cm (1½in) over it. Turn over, slip a length of raffia through under the top fold,

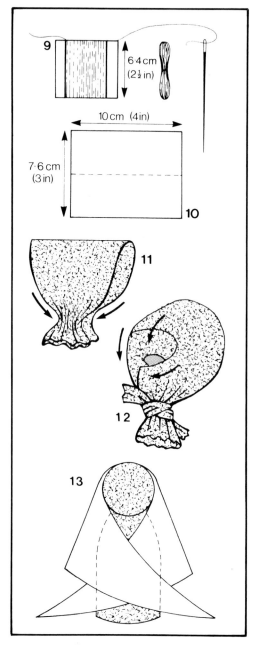

draw up slightly and tie round waist.

Hair. Cut a length of embroidery cotton 1.8m (2yd) for the hair. Wind this evenly round a 6.4cm (2½in) deep piece of card. Tie the loops at each side, then slide gently off the card and tie the centre *loosely* with cotton (Fig 9). Stick centre to top of head, then each side.

Cut the bonnet 7.6cm (3in) deep by 10cm (4in) wide (see Fig 10) and fold in half along the grain to measure 3.8cm (1½in) by 10cm (4in). Place round head, folded edge to the front, and gather the ends in to the neck at sides and back: then fold back edge down and each side towards the centre, sticking one over the other as in Fig 11. Tie round neck with raffia.

Mark two dots for eyes with black ink or felt pen.

OLD LADY GATHERING KINDLING

This is made in exactly the same way, but she wears a headscarf (Fig. 13) instead of a bonnet. It is simply a 7.6cm (3in) square of paper, folded diagonally: smear a little adhesive on the two front corners, twist them together, then pull the scarf gently over the head and stick at the back.

Her bundle of sticks is attached to her back by a length of raffia looped round each side, crossing over her chest and tied under one arm. Insert a length of pipe cleaner inside the upper half of the body to hold her bent position.

THE LITTLE GIRL

The little girl is made in just the same way as her mother, but the measurements are reduced.

BABY

The baby's head is made like the other dollies. Its body is several layers of maize.

*Decorative ideas which all
carry a breath of the countryside.*

Wooden spoon wall decorations

Wooden spoons like the one opposite can be made into pretty wall decorations to cheer up a kitchen or a breakfast room. Three decorated examples are shown on page 179 and a suggested method is given below.

Materials
Dried flowers, grasses, barley, oats, etc.
Ribbon, lace, etc., to trim.
Clear adhesive tape.
Thread to hang.

Method
Bunch together flower-heads, grasses, barley, etc., to fill bowl of spoon, cutting the stalks about 5cm (2in) long. Fit in place, then tape stalks securely to base of handle to hold in position.

Bunch together more of the dried materials, cut stalks as before, and tape further up the handle to cover previous tape. Continue in this way, turning the final bunch in the other direction if you like (see largest spoon).

Make a small bow of ribbon, raffia, lace, etc., and stitch in position over final tape.

Hang by a loop of thread suspended from the top of the handle.

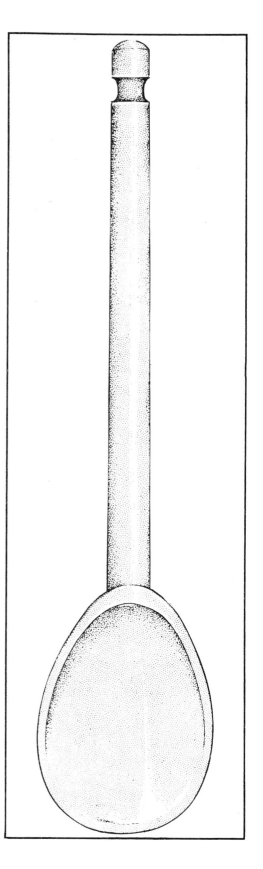

*A bookmark worthy the
rich tooling of a special book.*

Victorian
book-mark

The Victorians loved books, so they
needed book-marks – and these, of
course, were another excuse for
lavish decoration. Velvet ribbon is
used here with a pattern of seed
pearls based on guipure lace daisies.
But design should serve only as an
example: moire or satin ribbon would
be equally suitable, and any pretty
lace could form the basis for a
pattern of tiny coloured beads, sequins, etc. – or you could use a fine
braid. The arrangement you will find
dictated by your own choice of
materials – and your imagination.

Materials
30cm (12in) ribbon and lace or braid.
60cm (24in) narrow lace
to edge (optional).
Pearls, beads, sequins, etc.
Fabric adhesive.

Method
Turn under and stick the raw edge
at each end of the ribbon. Then stick
or stitch the lace down the centre.
Using the lace as a basis for your
design, stitch pearls, beads, sequins,
etc. over and beside it as illustrated,
decorating the bottom attractively
with a fringe, tassel or as shown.
Stick narrow lace to the back of the
ribbon so that it overlaps the side
edges.

181

*Summery pomanders, a harvest
collage and candles for winter.*

Statice pomander balls

Mementoes of the scented pomanders of earlier centuries have been combined here in a dried-flower pomander ball to hang beside a window, on a bedroom wall, or from the mirror of a dainty dressing table.

The ball is simplicity itself to make, needing only the styrofoam base, dried flower-heads - and patience. But stabbing the stalks home and watching the massed petals gradually spread over the surface of the ball is such a fascinating and relaxing occupation that one doesn't have time to become bored.

Almost any small flower can be substituted, and styrofoam balls can be obtained in at least three sizes: they are sold by florists and the artificial flower departments of large stores.

Method

Break or cut the flower-heads to leave 6–13mm ($\frac{1}{4}$–$\frac{1}{2}$in) of stalk, then push the dry stalk into the styrofoam until the base of the petals is against the surface. If you have difficulty pushing them in, or the stalks break, make a small hole first with the point of a small pair of scissors or a darning needle.

To attach ribbon, push a hairpin into the ball, leaving about 1.3cm ($\frac{1}{2}$in) protruding: thread ribbon through.

Pomander of dried flowers.

*Lavender and pot pourri, old ideas which
have lost none of their charm.*

Lavender sachets

These used to be made of fine muslin trimmed with hand-made lace. But the lavender and pot-pourri sachets shown here are in more practical nylon organdie, with machine-made nylon lace. For pot-pourri recipes, see the dried flower chapter.

Materials (for each sachet)
Two 6.4cm (2½in) squares of nylon organdie.
23cm (¼yd) gathered lace, 1.3cm (½in) wide.
9cm (3½in) narrow velvet or satin ribbon, lace motif or artificial flower spray to trim.
Dried lavender or pot-pourri.

Method
Stitch the gathered lace all round one piece of fabric, *on the right side,* 6mm (¼in) from the edge, with the decorative edge towards the centre of the square.
Tack the two pieces of fabric together, right sides inside, then join along three sides, following the previous stitching line. Trim seams, clip corners and turn to the right side.
Fill with lavender or pot-pourri, then turn in the remaining raw edges and slip-stitch together.
Make a tiny ribbon bow and stitch this or alternative trimming at one corner of the sachet.

Lavender from the garden.

Collage ingredients include pulse,
pasta and pearl barley.

Summer collage

Try raiding the store cupboard for dried pulse vegetables and pasta – the string box providing the stalks, with dishcloth cotton edging the leaves. The result could be a highly stylized flower collage.

Materials
Butter beans.
Split yellow peas.
Split green peas.
Pearl barley.
Spaghetti.
String.
Dishcloth knitting yarn.
A piece of heavy card.
Brown linen-type fabric, 2.5cm (1in) larger all round than the card.
Strong adhesive tape.
Clear all-purpose adhesive.
Adhesive tabs or rings to hang.

Method
Cover the card with fabric, allowing the excess to overlap equally all round: turn over each side and tape raw edges neatly to the back, trimming and turning in the corners neatly.
Very roughly work out your design before you begin, taking into consideration the shape of your picture background, and the materials you are using.

Arrange six butter beans in a 5cm (2in) diameter circle just above the centre of the vertical panel, and stick them in position. Fill the centre in with split green peas – always using plenty of adhesive.
Then cut a petal shape in paper, and draw round it six times, using a white crayon, to form the flower.
Encircle the butter beans, pick out the edge of the petals and make a line up the centre of each, with split yellow peas. Using lots of adhesive, fill in each petal by sprinkling pearl barley liberally over it and patting it down – shaking off the excess afterwards.
The upper flower is five butter beans, a green pea and an edging of yellow peas, forming a 6.4cm (2½in) diameter flower – with strips of spaghetti between the petals.
The lower flower is made up of a circle of nine butter beans around a green pea centre, making a 7cm (2¾in) diameter flower.
Design your leaf shape on paper, then cut it out and arrange it in position to balance the flowers – then draw round it as before, drawing in linking stalks at the same time. These are picked out in heavy parcel string (or you could use piping cord), with a thinner string for the two small flowers. Stick dishcloth yarn over the leaf outlines, then fill them in with bright green peas.
Fix tabs or rings at the back to hang.
The collage is now complete.

Embroidery

Origami

Soft Toys

Pottery

Dried Flowers

Filography

Macramé

Special Techniques

Craftsmith Shops

216-218 The Marlowes
Hemel Hempstead
Herts HP1 1BH

18 George Street
Richmond
Surrey

145 High Street
Southend-on-Sea
Essex

Guildhall Development
Exeter
Devon

18-20 Listergate
Nottingham

170 High Street
Slough SL1 1JN

29 Union Street
Birmingham B2 4LR

Other Useful Suppliers

Arts and Crafts
10 Byram Street
Huddersfield HD1 LDA

Dryad Ltd
Northgates
Leicester LE1 4OR

Also at
178 High Street
Kensington
London W8

Leisurecraft Centre
Search Press Ltd
2-10 Jerdan Place
London SW6 5PT

Craft Technique
19 Old Orchard Street
Bath

ACKNOWLEDGEMENTS

Thanks to Winifred Butler for material from NEEDLEWORK published by Pan Books Ltd in 1976; to June Field for material from CREATIVE PATCHWORK published by Pitman Publishing Ltd in 1974, and Pan Books Ltd 1976; to Evangeline Shears and Diantha Fielding for material from APPLIQUE published by Watson-Guptill Publications in the United States and Canada in 1972 and simultaneously in Great Britain by Pitman Publishing Ltd, and by Pan Books Ltd in 1974; to Mary Carey for material from CANDLE-MAKING published by Western Publishing Co. Inc. 1972, and Pan Books Ltd 1973; to Kunihiko Kasahara for material from CREATIVE ORIGAMI published by Japan Publications Inc. 1967, and Pitman Publishing Ltd 1970; to Mabs Tyler for material from THE BIG BOOK OF SOFT TOYS published by Wolfe Publishing Ltd in 1972, and by Pan Books Ltd in 1974 as two books, SOFT TOYS and MORE SOFT TOYS; also to Jolyon Hofsted for material from POTTERY published by Western Publishing Co. Inc. 1967 and Pan Books Ltd 1969; to Pamela Westland and Paula Critchley for material from DRIED AND PRESSED FLOWERS published by Ward Lock Ltd 1974 and Pan Books Ltd 1975; to Douglas K. Dix for material from FILOGRAPHY published by Pan Books Ltd 1975; to Mary Walker Phillips for material from MACRAME published by Western Publishing Co. Inc. 1970 and Pan Books Ltd 1972; and finally to Valerie Janitch for material from HANDMADE AT HOME published by Ward Lock Ltd 1973 and by Pan Books Ltd 1974 under the title COUNTRY CRAFTS.